Bluegrass Gatherings

Entertaining Through Kentucky's Seasons

Junior League of Louisville

Bluegrass Gatherings

Entertaining Through Kentucky's Seasons

Copyright © 2013 by
Junior League of Louisville, Inc.
982 Eastern Parkway
Suite 7
Louisville, Kentucky 40217
www.juniorleaguelouisville.org

Photography © by Fred Minnick except as noted
Collage Photography © by M. A. Buckner (pages 15, 61,109, and 153)
Collage Layouts by PriceWeber

Manufactured and Produced by

 Favorite Recipes® Press

An imprint of

 SOUTHWESTERN Publishing Group

P.O. Box 305142, Nashville, Tennessee 37230
1-800-358-0560

Art Director and Book Design: Steve Newman
Project Manager: Julee Hicks
Editorial Director: Mary Cummings

Library of Congress Control Number: 2012947745
ISBN: 978-0-9613330-2-7

Manufactured in the United States of America
First Printing: 2013
7,500 copies

Bluegrass Gatherings

Entertaining Through Kentucky's Seasons

Junior League of Louisville

Contents

Spring

Summer

Contents

Fall

Winter

Forewords

Spring

There are few places better in the world than Kentucky in the spring. At our historic home, Poplar Terrace, the breeze from the mighty Ohio River is cool, and the scent of fresh mint perfumes the air, with beauty and happiness abounding as the daily wonders of nature magically reappear. Kentucky's magnificent natural beauty motivates each of us to open our hearts and our homes to friends, visitors, and family alike for delicious food and the finest Kentucky bourbon, flowing at Poplar Terrace from our handcrafted mint julep fountain. Kentucky's beloved spring season inspires each of us to show our joy in caring for and sharing with one another all of which results in the very best of southern hospitality!

—Christina Lee Brown, Founder of The Festival of Faiths

Summer

Summer on a farm in Kentucky is abundant with lush pastures and gardens bursting with delectable things to eat. It is the time of year when it is easy to see what our Commonwealth really is—our state's fertility. We must learn to be a people that value it and sustain it because it is, in fact, our common health.

—Mary Berry, Executive Director of the Berry Center

Fall

My culinary roots and inspiration have been directly influenced by my life growing up on a large farm surrounded by people who loved to cook and who gathered what they needed from our large garden and orchard. Each season has its particular standouts, and the fall bounty is hard-wired for its staying power and its succulence. Nothing beats the rich colors of the eggplant and the myriad varieties of apples, and the squash, if chosen fresh from nature, have aroma and taste unparalleled.

—Kathy Cary, Owner and Chef of Lilly's—A Kentucky Bistro

Winter

The knowledge of traditional foodways may be becoming lost in other places, but here in the Bluegrass there is still a love and respect for heirloom vegetables, heritage breeds of livestock, and recipes that have been handed down through generations of families. To plant and nurture a seed until the fruit is perfectly ripe to eat is a time-honored tradition that lives on. Each of the four seasons is a celebration of local food. The harmony between cook and garden is genuine.

—Mark Williams, Southern Regional Governor, Slow Food USA

GARDEN • COOK • ENJOY

How on earth does a New York City boy end up writing the foreword to a Kentucky cookbook? Yup, it's true. I'm a Yank. Growing up just a few miles from Times Square, my youth was filled with Sunday pasta and Italian pastries, Chinatown specialties on trips downtown, and potato pancakes and kugel in the homes of my Jewish friends. Not exactly traditional Bluegrass cuisine.

But rather than being raised with a silver spoon in my mouth, I grew up with a wooden spoon in my hand. Whether it was fresh tomatoes and corn from my father's vegetable garden, just picked peaches from DePiero's Farm, homemade apple pie, lasagna, or my mother's famous sour cream coffee cake, my childhood years were spent in our family kitchen. Along with my brothers and sisters, I slowly absorbed my mother's kitchen secrets and talents through her loving preparation of daily meals, holiday feasts, and birthday treats. And beyond the immediate family, all visiting relatives and friends knew well that a warm welcome was always followed by a choice—potato peeler or masher!

As a gardener by vocation and avocation I was in Seventh Heaven when 15 years ago my wife, son, and I moved from Maine to Kentucky—an increase in the growing season from 90 days to 180—so much more time to grow tomatoes! And during those last fifteen years, I had the distinct pleasure and sheer joy to watch several things happen. First, my son, who was just four years old at the time of the move, discovered gardening and cooking. During fabulously long Kentucky springs, he grew sugar snap and snow peas, nurtured the vines, and delighted in picking a handful each evening for the dinner table. We baked bread weekly—experimenting with recipes from across the street and around the globe. He eventually graduated to pastries—éclairs, napoleons, and the like that have become new family traditions.

But during that time, another food development was emerging throughout Louisville and across Kentucky. The community as a whole rediscovered good, fresh, and local food, and food traditions that had been there all along began to become mainstream. Farmers' markets popped up all across the Bluegrass. Local vegetable farmers, cheese crafters, beer brewers—heck, even soy sauce magicians— began to spread across the land like a sultry Kentucky summer. And that movement paired with Kentucky's deep history is illustrated nowhere better than in the selection of the four seasonal writers included in these pages: Christina Lee Brown and the Brown family's unrivaled position in the Kentucky bourbon industry; Mary Berry and the Berry family's tradition of preserving our precious Bluegrass land and inspiring others to do the same; the incomparable Kathy Cary of Lilly's—one of the best in the food business who just happens to have deep, deep roots in the garden and Kentucky tradition; and Mark Williams, who can only be described as Kentucky's pied piper of good, fresh, and local food—with a love of heritage recipes and ingredients thrown in for good measure.

At Yew Dell Botanical Gardens, we've been happy to contribute our part to both the rediscovery of home-/local-grown food and keeping alive and sharing traditional Kentucky recipes. Through gardening classes, traditional cooking workshops, and more, we're honored to be part of the rebirth of good, fresh, local, and traditional food.

So there you have it. I may be a New Yorker by birth, but Kentucky grows on a soul quickly and irreversibly. And while the Cappiello household still delights in a Sunday lasagna dinner and cannoli dessert, corn pudding and bourbon bread pudding are now held in places of high regard!

—*Paul E. Cappiello, Ph.D., Executive Director, Yew Dell Botanical Gardens, Crestwood, Kentucky*

About the Cookbook

A Handcrafted Mint Julep Fountain

The Bluegrass State is often associated with thoroughbred racing, kind-hearted hospitality, the world's finest bourbon, and delectable, southern cuisine. These rich Kentucky traditions—highlighted in *Bluegrass Gatherings: Entertaining through Kentucky's Seasons*—will set the stage for your own gatherings of family and friends.

Bluegrass Gatherings, the fourth cookbook published by the Junior League of Louisville (JLL), includes lush menus—celebrating local events and daily life—and timeless photographs. Most of the recipes originated from the kitchens of League members, family, friends, and many well-known local chefs. Whether you're cooking for one or twenty, our hope is that this book inspires you to buy local, cook often, and gather for any occasion.

Concurrent to our city's local food movement, this cookbook features a seasonal, menu-based cooking experience. Fresh, local ingredients are woven into mouthwatering recipes, local farm highlights provide a road map for the lush bounty of the Commonwealth, and the Kentucky Produce Buying Guide tells you when this beautiful produce is available.

By sharing the recipes in *Bluegrass Gatherings*, you are helping the Junior League of Louisville continue our commitment to community service and our members. Proceeds from our cookbooks go toward community projects, training volunteers, and the development of women in our community. Our recipe for future success includes you. For this, we thank you.

—*Bluegrass Gatherings* Committee

 Beverage Kentucky  JLL Favorite  Fast Track

About the League

Over ninety years ago a group of ten women met to discuss the need for a volunteer organization in Louisville. As a result, the Junior League of Louisville was formed in 1921 with fifty active members. While our membership has increased significantly, community service remains the heart of the Junior League.

Over the years, League members have contributed countless hours of community service to influence thousands of lives through their hands-on projects. The League has made an impact on the community by establishing scholarship funds and well-baby clinics and developing a Children's Theater now known as Stage One. The League also played an integral role in revitalizing a section of downtown Louisville, establishing the Ronald McDonald House and Youth Career Development Center, and creating Noogieland—a children's program at Gilda's Club that is designed to meet the needs of children touched by cancer.

Today the JLL's community projects include: Done-In-A-Day (various community projects that are completed in one day), Bloom Boutique (an event that outfits select high school women for prom, giving them the self confidence and tools they need to enjoy this special milestone), Urban Garden (a project developed to unite communities and organizations with sustainable life practices), Gilda's Club (a partnership to help serve people whose lives have been affected by cancer), Family Scholar House (cooking classes that assist single parent residents to help understand the fundamentals of healthy cooking), and Keep In Touch (a JLL project made possible by Susan G. Komen for the Cure that provides support to women diagnosed with breast cancer).

In addition to community service, leadership development through training is a key focus of the League. Through community placements and projects, opportunities to lead on committee boards, and leadership development seminars, our members achieve invaluable experience that is carried with them in everyday work and life.

The JLL is proud to be part of a mission that extends to over 155,000 women in 292 Leagues across four countries who make a difference in their communities every day through their volunteer efforts. As you will see in the pages ahead, the JLL has a rich history in Louisville. As we approach our 100th year, it will be exciting to see how we continue to be a catalyst for community change!

—The Junior League of Louisville

Mission Statement: *JLL is an organization of women committed to promoting voluntarism, to developing the potential of women, and to improving the community through the effective action and leadership of trained volunteers. Its purpose is exclusively educational and charitable.*

Season / Chapter Sponsors

Spring: Heaven Hill Distilleries, Inc. www.heavenhill.com

Summer: Lauren Adams Ogden

Fall: Yum! Brands Foundation www.yum.com

Winter: White Clay Consulting www.whiteclay.com

Menu Sponsors

Jamie Estes, Estes Public Relations www.estespr.com

Louisville Stoneware www.louisvillestoneware.com

Churchill Downs www.churchilldowns.com

North End Cafe www.northendcafe.com

Colonial Designs www.colonialdesigns.net

Maggie M. Heely, Event Warriors and Weekend Wedding Warriors
www.myweddingwarrior.com

Solberg Manufacturing Inc. www.solbergmfg.com

PriceWeber www.priceweber.com

M.A. Buckner www.mabuckner.com

Kentucky Proud www.kyproud.com

Bittners www.bittners.com

Algood Food Company www.algoodfood.com

Foxhollow Farm www.foxhollow.com

Mint Julep Cake

Spring

St. Charles Exchange

Spring

The courtyard of St. Charles Exchange offers a rustic yet upscale ambience in one of the oldest buildings in downtown Louisville's trendy West Main Street District. Exposed brick gives a polished contrast to the collection of fragrant hydrangeas, roses, and assorted greenery that casually line the center of this table setting. Napkins arranged in guests' wine glasses are a memorable detail that is perfect for any occasion when wine will be served. Tea lights allow for an effortless transition from day to dusk, especially in the late spring.

SPRING MENUS

MARCH MADNESS 16

APRIL SHOWERS BRING MAY FLOWERS 22

THUNDER COOKOUT 30

LILIES FOR THE FILLIES COCKTAIL PARTY 38

RUN FOR THE ROSES BRUNCH 48

Spring Chapter Sponsored by
Heaven Hill Distilleries, Inc.

HEAVEN HILL
DISTILLERIES, INC.

March Madness

Serves 6

Buffalo and Blue Meatballs

Tip-off Poppers

3-Point BLT Salad

Chipotle and Cheese Corn Bread Biscuits

Out of Bounds Spicy Pork and Hominy Stew

Final Four Turtle Bars

Paloma

Chipotle and Cheese Corn Bread Biscuits

BUFFALO AND BLUE MEATBALLS

1 tablespoon vegetable oil
1/4 cup (1/2 stick) unsalted butter
1/3 cup hot red pepper sauce
1 pound ground chicken, preferably thighs
1 egg
1/4 cup finely chopped celery
1 cup soft bread crumbs
1/2 teaspoon celery salt
1/2 teaspoon smoked paprika
1/2 teaspoon salt

Serves 6

BLUE CHEESE DIPPING SAUCE

1/2 cup buttermilk
1/2 cup plain Greek yogurt
2/3 cup crumbled good-quality blue cheese
1 tablespoon cider vinegar
1 teaspoon Worcestershire sauce
1/2 teaspoon lemon juice
1/2 teaspoon white pepper
1/4 teaspoon cumin
1/4 cup (about) milk

Coat an 8×8-inch baking dish evenly with the vegetable oil. Melt the butter in a small saucepan. Stir in the hot sauce. Cook over low heat until hot, stirring constantly. Remove from the heat and cool completely. Combine the chicken, egg, celery, bread crumbs, celery salt, paprika, salt and hot sauce mixture in a bowl and mix well with clean hands. Chill for 30 minutes. Shape the mixture into 1-inch balls and fit snugly into the prepared baking dish. Bake in a preheated 450-degree oven for 20 minutes or until firm and cooked through. Cool for 5 minutes before serving with the blue cheese dipping sauce.

Combine the buttermilk, yogurt, cheese, vinegar, Worcestershire sauce, lemon juice, white pepper and cumin in a bowl and mix well. Stir in the milk, a few tablespoons at a time, until the sauce is thick but pourable. Chill, covered, for 12 to 36 hours before serving.

The Commonwealth is well known for its love of basketball. Two of the most storied programs in college basketball, and in-state rivals, the University of Louisville and the University of Kentucky have celebrated multiple NCAA championships and Final Four appearances. Other state schools—Western Kentucky University, Murray State University, and Morehead State University, among others—make regular appearances in the NCAA tournament. Celebrate the Bluegrass State's love of basketball with a March Madness party and watch things heat up in the kitchen and on the court.

TIP-OFF POPPERS

20 fresh jalapeño chiles
10 ounces cream cheese, softened
1 pound regular sliced bacon, crisp-cooked
  and crumbled
1/2 cup barbecue sauce

Serves 10

Variation: You may use fontina, Monterey Jack, Havarti or goat cheese instead of cream cheese.

*C*ut the jalapeño chiles in half lengthwise and remove the seeds and white membrane with a small spoon. Leave a small amount of seeds and white membrane if you prefer more spice.

Fill each jalapeño chile half with equal portions of the cream cheese. Arrange on a greased 10×15-inch baking pan. Bake in a preheated 350-degree oven for 16 minutes. Top each with equal potions of the bacon and barbecue sauce. Bake for 7 minutes longer. Serve warm or at room temperature.

Note: Wear food-handling gloves when working with hot chiles.

3-POINT BLT SALAD

8 ounces bacon
1/3 cup Catalina salad dressing
1/2 teaspoon mustard
Dash of salt
Dash of pepper
8 cups spinach, torn into bite-size pieces
2 tomatoes, cut into bite-size pieces
1/2 cup (2 ounces) shredded sharp
  Cheddar cheese

Serves 8

*C*ook the bacon in a skillet until crisp. Remove to paper towels to drain, reserving 2 tablespoons of bacon drippings in the skillet. Crumble the bacon. Add the salad dressing, mustard, salt and pepper to the drippings and mix well. Cook over low heat until heated through, stirring constantly. Combine the spinach, tomatoes, cheese and bacon in a salad bowl. Drizzle the dressing over the top and toss gently to coat. Serve immediately.

Variation: You may use crumbled blue cheese or feta cheese instead of Cheddar cheese. You may also use reduced-calorie salad dressing.

CHIPOTLE AND CHEESE CORN BREAD BISCUITS

1 tablespoon unsalted butter
3/4 cup chopped green onions
1 1/2 cups all-purpose flour
1/2 cup yellow cornmeal
2 tablespoons sugar
2 1/2 teaspoons baking powder
3/4 teaspoon kosher salt
1/2 teaspoon baking soda
1/2 cup (1 stick) cold unsalted butter,
    cut into 1/2-inch cubes
1 1/2 cups (6 ounces) shredded extra-sharp
    yellow Cheddar cheese
1 egg
3/4 cup (about) buttermilk
1 tablespoon finely chopped canned
    chipotle chiles in adobo sauce
1 egg
1 tablespoon whipping cream

Serves 10

*M*elt 1 tablespoon butter in a nonstick skillet over medium heat. Add the green onions and sauté for 2 minutes. Remove to a bowl.

Combine the flour, cornmeal, sugar, baking powder, salt and baking soda in a food processor and process just until mixed. Add 1/2 cup cold butter and pulse until the mixture resembles coarse crumbs. Add the cheese and pulse just until mixed. Remove to a bowl.

Whisk 1 egg in a 1-cup glass measuring cup. Stir in enough buttermilk to make 1 cup. Stir in the green onion mixture and chipotle chiles.

Make a well in the center of the flour mixture. Pour the buttermilk mixture into the well and stir just until mixed. Knead the dough on a generously floured surface about 10 turns or just until the dough holds together. Pat 3/4-inch thick and cut with a 3-inch biscuit cutter.

Arrange the biscuits 1 inch apart on an ungreased baking sheet. Beat 1 egg and the cream in a small bowl and brush over the tops of the biscuits. Bake in a preheated 425-degree oven for 18 minutes or until golden brown and firm and a wooden pick inserted in the center comes out clean. Remove to a wire rack to cool for 5 minutes. Serve warm.

Note: These are great served with soup or chili.

PALOMA

2 ounces Lunazul Blanco Tequila
Splash of lime juice
Pinch of salt
6 ounces grapefruit soda
Lime wedge for garnish

Serves 1

*C*ombine the tequila, lime juice and salt in a tall glass with ice. Top off with the grapefruit soda and stir gently to mix. Garnish with a lime wedge.

OUT OF BOUNDS SPICY PORK AND HOMINY STEW

2 tablespoons ancho chili powder
2 teaspoons dried oregano
1 1/2 teaspoons smoked paprika
1 1/2 teaspoons ground cumin
1/2 teaspoon salt
1/4 teaspoon pepper
1 (1 1/2-pound) pork tenderloin, trimmed and
   cut into 1/2-inch cubes
3 teaspoons olive oil
2 cups chopped onions
1 green bell pepper, chopped
1 red bell pepper, chopped
1 tablespoon minced garlic
2 1/2 cups fat-free, low-sodium chicken broth
1 (28-ounce) can hominy, drained
1 (14-ounce) can fire-roasted diced tomatoes

Serves 6

Combine the chili powder, oregano, paprika, cumin, salt and pepper in a large bowl and mix well. Reserve 1 1/2 teaspoons of the seasoning mixture. Add the pork to the remaining seasoning mixture and toss to coat.

Heat 2 teaspoons of the olive oil in a heavy saucepan over medium-high heat. Add the pork and sauté for 5 minutes or until brown. Remove the pork to a bowl using a slotted spoon. Add the remaining 1 teaspoon olive oil to the saucepan. Add the onions, green bell pepper, red bell pepper and garlic and sauté for 5 minutes or until the vegetables are tender. Stir in the pork, reserved 1 1/2 teaspoons seasoning mixture, broth, hominy and tomatoes and bring to a boil. Reduce the heat. Simmer, partially covered, for 25 minutes.

FINAL FOUR TURTLE BARS

2 cups all-purpose flour
1/2 cup confectioners' sugar
1 cup (2 sticks) unsalted butter, softened
1 egg
1 (14-ounce) can sweetened condensed milk
1 teaspoon vanilla extract
1 cup pecans, coarsely chopped
3/4 cup chocolate chips
1 cup toffee bits

Makes 15

Combine the flour, confectioners' sugar and butter in a food processor and pulse until the mixture resembles coarse crumbs. Pat over the bottom of a greased 9×13-inch baking pan. Bake in a preheated 350-degree oven for 13 minutes or until golden brown. Whisk the egg, sweetened condensed milk and vanilla in a bowl. Pour over the baked crust. Sprinkle with the pecans, chocolate chips and toffee bits. Bake for 25 minutes longer or until the filling is set and the edges are golden brown. Remove to a wire rack to cool completely. Chill for 2 hours before cutting into bars.

April Showers Bring May Flowers

Serves 6

"I Do" Strawberry Bruschetta

Blissful Blini with Arugula and Shallots

Jumbo Lump Crab with
Avocado, Green Goddess Dressing and Mango Salsa

Perfect Pair Penne

Lavender Lemon Chiffon Cupcakes with
Blackberry Buttercream

Honeymoon Raspberry Mousse

Bubbles and Blue

April Showers Bring May Flowers Menu Sponsored by
Jamie Estes, Estes Public Relations

"I Do" Strawberry Bruschetta

"I Do" Strawberry Bruschetta

1 crusty French baguette, cut into
  1/2-inch slices
2 tablespoons olive oil
2 1/2 cups chopped strawberries
2 tablespoons chopped fresh mint or basil
1/2 cup balsamic vinegar
1 teaspoon sugar
2 tablespoons olive oil

Serves 8 to 10

*B*rush both sides of the bread slices lightly with 2 tablespoons olive oil and arrange on a baking sheet. Bake in a preheated 325-degree oven for 3 to 5 minutes. Turn over the bread and bake for 3 to 5 minutes longer or until lightly toasted. Remove the bread to a wire rack to cool.

Mix the strawberries and mint in a bowl and set aside. Cook the vinegar and sugar in a saucepan over medium heat until reduced to 1/4 cup, stirring constantly. Remove from the heat and let cool. Add the cooled vinegar and 2 tablespoons olive oil to the strawberries and toss to mix. Spoon equal portions of the strawberry mixture onto the bread slices and serve immediately.

Variation: Crumbled feta can be added for additional color and flavor.

*B*loom Boutique—an annual event hosted by The Junior League of Louisville—aids in making prom more than just a night of dancing for select young ladies in the community. Guests are treated to an enjoyable day of shopping, makeovers, and pampering, giving them the tools and self-confidence they need to make their high school formal a memorable experience. New and like-new dresses, handbags, jewelry, and time are donated by local businesses, people in the community, and League members.

BLISSFUL BLINI WITH ARUGULA AND SHALLOTS

BLINI

2 eggs
1 tablespoon sugar
1/3 heaping teaspoon salt
1 cup all-purpose flour
2 1/2 cups buttermilk

Makes 3 dozen

ARUGULA AND SHALLOT TOPPING

2 tablespoons butter
4 shallots, chopped
1 tablespoon sugar
1/2 cup sour cream
1 teaspoon horseradish
2 cups arugula

Whisk the eggs, sugar and salt in a bowl. Sift the flour over the top and then whisk into the egg mixture. Whisk in the buttermilk until smooth. Heat a griddle or skillet over medium heat. Spray with nonstick cooking spray or lightly oil the griddle or skillet.

Pour 1 tablespoon of batter into the pan. Turn the blini over when the edges look crisp and the center appears dry. Cook for 1 to 2 minutes longer or until light brown. Remove to a plate and keep warm. Repeat with the remaining batter.

Melt the butter in a skillet. Add the shallots and sauté until golden brown. Stir in the sugar and reduce the heat to medium-low. Cook until the shallots are a caramel color. Remove from the heat.

Mix the sour cream and horseradish in a bowl. Spoon a dollop of the sour cream mixture onto each blini and top with 1/2 teaspoon of the shallots. Sprinkle evenly with arugula and serve.

JUMBO LUMP CRAB WITH AVOCADO, GREEN GODDESS DRESSING AND MANGO SALSA

GREEN GODDESS DRESSING

1 anchovy fillet
1/3 cup mayonnaise
2 tablespoons sour cream
1/4 cup buttermilk
1 teaspoon minced chives
1/2 teaspoon chopped fresh basil
1 teaspoon minced tarragon
1 tablespoon chopped flat-leaf parsley
1 1/2 teaspoons minced shallots
Juice of 1/2 lemon
Salt and pepper to taste
1 pound jumbo lump crab meat

MANGO SALSA AND ASSEMBLY

1 fresh mango, cut into 1/4-inch pieces
1 teaspoon chopped fresh jalapeño chile
1 tablespoon chopped red bell pepper
1 tablespoon chopped yellow bell pepper
1/2 red onion, minced
1/2 teaspoon minced fresh garlic
Juice of 1 lime
1 teaspoon minced fresh cilantro
Salt and pepper to taste
2 large avocados, cut into 1/2-inch pieces
4 cups micro greens or baby greens

Serves 6

*S*oak the anchovy in a bowl of cold water; drain. Place in a small baking pan and dry in the oven on low heat. Coarsely chop the anchovy. Whisk the anchovy, mayonnaise, sour cream, buttermilk, chives, basil, tarragon, parsley, shallots, lemon juice, salt and pepper in a bowl. Add the desired amount of dressing to the crab meat in a bowl; mix well. Keep chilled until ready to serve.

*C*ombine the mango, jalapeño chile, red bell pepper, yellow bell pepper, onion, garlic, lime juice, cilantro, salt and pepper in a bowl and mix well. Place a 3-inch tian mold on each of 6 plates.

Layer half the crab mixture in equal portions into each mold. Top each with one-sixth of the avocado, one-sixth of the mango salsa and equal portions of the remaining crab mixture. Top each with micro greens.

Chef: Chef Dean Corbett, Corbett's—an American place

PERFECT PAIR PENNE

Grated zest of 1 lemon
1 1/2 cups dry white wine
1 cup heavy cream
1 bunch asparagus, trimmed and
    cut into 1-inch pieces
16 ounces penne
3 tablespoons butter, cut into pieces
Juice of 1 lemon
1/2 teaspoon kosher salt
1 teaspoon freshly ground pepper
4 ounces grated Parmesan cheese
1 tablespoon extra-virgin olive oil
Kosher salt and freshly ground pepper to taste

Serves 4 to 6

Bring the lemon zest and wine to a boil in a nonreactive saucepan. Reduce the heat to medium and cook for 10 minutes or until thickened. Remove from the heat and stir in half the cream. Stir in the remaining cream. Return to the heat and bring to a boil. Reduce the heat and simmer for 5 minutes or until the mixture is thickened and slightly reduced. Remove from the heat.

Bring a large saucepan of water to a boil and add the asparagus. Cook for 1 minute. Remove the asparagus with a slotted spoon to a bowl of ice water to stop the cooking process; drain. Add the pasta to the boiling water and cook according to the package directions. Drain the pasta, reserving 1 cup of the cooking liquid. Return the drained pasta to the saucepan on the stove.

Add the cream mixture, butter, lemon juice, 1/2 teaspoon salt, 1 teaspoon pepper, asparagus, 1/2 cup of the reserved cooking liquid and the cheese to the pasta and toss to mix. Add additional cooking liquid if the mixture is too thick.

Divide the pasta among 4 to 6 plates and drizzle equal portions of the olive oil over the top of the pasta. Season with salt and pepper to taste. Serve immediately.

LAVENDER LEMON CHIFFON CUPCAKES WITH BLACKBERRY BUTTERCREAM

CUPCAKES

1³/4 cups (227g) cake flour
2 teaspoons (10g) baking powder
³/4 teaspoon (74ml) salt
1/3 cup (74ml) vegetable oil
1/3 cup (100g) simple syrup
Grated zest of 2 lemons
1/4 cup (60ml) lemon juice
1/2 teaspoon dried lavender
6 egg yolks (100g), at room temperature
1/4 cup (53g) sugar
6 egg whites (170g), at room temperature
³/4 cup (160g) sugar
1/4 teaspoon cream of tartar
Blackberry Buttercream (below)

Serves 12 to 18

BLACKBERRY BUTTERCREAM

1¹/3 cups (266g) organic sugar
5 tablespoons (75ml) water
5 egg whites (150g)
2/3 cup (134g) organic sugar
1³/4 cups (3¹/2 sticks) (400g) European-style
   butter, softened
1/2 cup (100g) blackberry purée, blackberry
   preserves or fresh blackberries

Serves 12 to 18

Chef: Chef Claudia Delatorre, Cake Flour—
A Natural Baking Company

Sift the cake flour, baking powder and salt together. Whisk the oil, simple syrup, lemon zest, lemon juice and lavender flavoring in a bowl. Beat the egg yolks and 1/4 cup sugar in a mixing bowl at high speed until pale yellow and tripled in volume. Beat in the lemon mixture at low speed. Fold in the dry ingredients. Whisk the egg whites, ³/4 cup sugar and the cream of tartar in a bowl until medium stiff peaks form; do not overmix. Fold into the batter. Fill paper-lined muffin cups two-thirds full. Bake in a preheated 350-degree oven for 16 to 18 minutes or until a wooden pick inserted in the center comes out clean. Cool a wire rack. Frost with the blackberry buttercream.

Cook 1¹/3 cups sugar and the water in a saucepan over medium heat to 220 degrees on a candy thermometer. Beat the egg whites and 2/3 cup sugar in a mixing bowl at high speed until stiff peaks form. Pour the hot syrup slowly down the side of the mixing bowl, beating at low speed. Beat in the butter gradually at medium speed. Beat until smooth. Beat in the preserves.

Notes: Do not be afraid of the metric system. It is friendly and very accurate. Using the metric system will always give you the correct amount no matter what time of year (weather influences ingredient weights, from winter to summer, etc.). Invest in a scale; you will be glad you did.

These cupcakes also make a perfect party favor for guests!

HONEYMOON RASPBERRY MOUSSE

8 ounces mascarpone cheese, softened
1/2 cup raspberry jam
1/2 teaspoon vanilla extract
1 cup heavy whipping cream
3 tablespoons confectioners' sugar
1 cup fresh raspberries for garnish
Mint leaves for garnish

Serves 4 to 6

Beat the cheese, jam and vanilla in a mixing bowl until light and fluffy. Beat the cream and confectioners' sugar in a mixing bowl until soft peaks form.

Fold the whipped cream into the cheese mixture in batches. Spoon into serving dishes and chill for 1 hour. Garnish with the raspberries and mint leaves and serve.

Note: Serve this at your next cocktail party in 2-ounce serving dishes with a small tasting spoon placed in each dish.

BUBBLES AND BLUE

2 ounces Hpnotiq liqueur, chilled
2 ounces Champagne, chilled

Serves 1

Pour the Hpnotiq and Champagne into a Champagne flute. Serve immediately.

Thunder Cookout

Serves 6

KENTUCKY BOURBON CARAMEL CORN

PICNIC PARTY PIZZAS

FESTIVAL FRIED CHICKEN

FIREWORKS MAC 'N' CHEESE

SUGAR SNAP PEA SALAD

COCONUT CREAM PIE

PLANTATION TEA

TEA IT UP

Thunder Cookout Menu Sponsored by

Louisville Stoneware

LOUISVILLE
STONEWARE
THE ART OF LIVING!

KENTUCKY CRAFTED   FOUNDED 1815

Festival Fried Chicken

KENTUCKY BOURBON CARAMEL CORN

20 cups popped popcorn
3 cups salted peanuts, almonds or pecans
1 cup (2 sticks) butter
2 cups packed brown sugar
1/2 cup corn syrup
1 teaspoon salt
1/2 teaspoon baking soda
1 teaspoon vanilla extract
3 tablespoons Kentucky bourbon,
    or to taste
8 ounces bacon, crisp-cooked and crumbled

Serves 4 to 6

Spread equal portions of the popcorn and peanuts into two large shallow baking pans. Melt the butter in a saucepan over medium heat. Stir in the brown sugar, corn syrup and salt. Bring to a boil, stirring constantly. Boil for 4 minutes without stirring.

Remove from the heat and stir in the baking soda, vanilla and bourbon. Pour equal portions in a thin stream over the popcorn and peanuts and stir gently to coat.

Bake in a preheated 250-degree oven for 40 minutes, stirring every 15 to 20 minutes. Add the bacon and stir to mix. Bake for 20 minutes longer. Remove to a wire rack to cool completely. Break into pieces when cool.

Note: For a different taste, sprinkle toasted coconut, mini chocolate chips, and/or chopped almonds over the warm popcorn mixture when removed from the oven.

PICNIC PARTY PIZZAS

5 pita breads
2 tablespoons olive oil
8 ounces cream cheese, softened
$1/2$ cup finely chopped white onion
2 garlic cloves, minced
1 tablespoon chopped fresh dill weed
$1/2$ teaspoon celery seeds
$1/4$ cup chopped red bell pepper
$1/4$ cup chopped yellow bell pepper
$1/4$ cup shredded carrots
$1/4$ cup finely chopped broccoli
$1/2$ cup (2 ounces) shredded mozzarella cheese
   or Cheddar cheese

Serves 6 to 8

Cut the pita bread into rounds using a 3-inch biscuit cutter. Brush the rounds with the olive oil and arrange on a baking sheet. Bake in a preheated 350-degree oven for 5 minutes, turning over halfway through baking. Remove to a wire rack to cool.

Combine the cream cheese, onion, garlic, dill weed and celery seeds in a bowl and mix well. Spread equal portions of the cream cheese mixture over the bread rounds. Top with equal portions of the red bell pepper, yellow bell pepper, carrots and broccoli and sprinkle with equal portions of the mozzarella cheese.

Serve chilled or arrange on a baking sheet and warm in the oven for 10 minutes or until the mozzarella cheese is melted.

Thunder Over Louisville is the annual kickoff event of the Kentucky Derby Festival. The day begins with one of the top five air shows in the nation. As the sun goes down, prepare to see the largest fireworks display in North America. First ignited in 1990, hundreds of thousands of people line the banks of the Ohio River each year to celebrate the start of a two-week celebration leading up to the Kentucky Derby.

FESTIVAL FRIED CHICKEN

1 1/2 *cups low-fat buttermilk*
2 *tablespoons finely chopped fresh parsley, or*
1 teaspoon parsley flakes
2 *tablespoons finely chopped fresh tarragon,*
or 2 teaspoons dried tarragon
1 *teaspoon onion powder*
1 *teaspoon cayenne pepper*
4 *chicken thighs*
4 *chicken legs*
1 *cup all-purpose flour*
1 1/2 *cups panko bread crumbs*
2 *teaspoons salt*
1/2 *teaspoon black pepper*
1/2 *teaspoon cayenne pepper*
1 *teaspoon onion powder*
3 *cups (about) vegetable oil*
Salt to taste

Serves 4 to 6

Variation: You may substitute any bone-in, skin-on chicken pieces for the legs and thighs. Adjust the cooking time accordingly.

Combine the buttermilk, parsley, tarragon, 1 teaspoon onion powder and 1 teaspoon cayenne pepper in a bowl and mix well. Pour into a large sealable plastic bag and add the chicken. Seal the bag and turn to coat.

Marinate in the refrigerator for 8 to 12 hours, turning at least once. Combine the flour, bread crumbs, 2 teaspoons salt, the black pepper, 1/2 teaspoon cayenne pepper and 1 teaspoon onion powder in a large sealable plastic bag. Seal the bag and shake to mix. Remove one piece of chicken from the marinade and allow the excess to drain. Place the chicken piece in the flour mixture and seal the bag. Turn the bag to coat the chicken. Remove the coated chicken to parchment paper. Repeat with the remaining chicken pieces. Let the coated chicken stand for 10 to 15 minutes. Coat each piece of chicken in the flour mixture again and return to the parchment paper.

Pour the oil into 2 heavy skillets to a depth of 3 to 4 inches. Heat the oil to 350 degrees. Add 4 pieces of chicken to each skillet and fry for 15 minutes. Turn the chicken over and fry for 10 to 15 minutes or until golden brown and cooked through. Keep the oil at 350 degrees during frying. Remove the chicken to a wire rack and immediately season with salt to taste.

Note: While it's impossible to beat the taste of the Colonel's Kentucky Fried Chicken, this recipe comes pretty close!

FIREWORKS MAC 'N' CHEESE

2 cups cottage cheese
1 cup sour cream
1 egg
1/2 teaspoon seasoned salt
1 tablespoon Worcestershire sauce
1/2 teaspoon pepper
1 teaspoon dry mustard
1 1/2 teaspoons onion powder
8 ounces ziti, cooked and drained
8 ounces shredded sharp Cheddar cheese
6 tablespoons panko bread crumbs
Red food coloring (optional)
Blue food coloring (optional)

Serves 6 to 8

Process the cottage cheese, sour cream, egg, seasoned salt, Worcestershire sauce, pepper, dry mustard and onion powder in a food processor or blender until smooth. Remove to a bowl and stir in the pasta.

Reserve 2 tablespoons of the Cheddar cheese and add the remaining Cheddar cheese to the pasta; mix well. Spoon into a greased 9×13-inch baking dish and sprinkle with the reserved Cheddar cheese.

Bake in a preheated 350-degree oven for 30 minutes or until golden brown.

Divide the bread crumbs equally among 3 small bowls. Mix red food coloring into one bowl of bread crumbs to the desired tint. Mix blue food coloring into another bowl of bread crumbs to the desired tint. Sprinkle the red, blue and plain white bread crumbs over the baked macaroni and cheese.

Note: This is a spin on traditional macaroni and cheese. The red, white and blue "sprinkles" add that little sparkle that's perfect for a cookout.

SUGAR SNAP PEA SALAD

8 ounces sugar snap peas
Salt to taste
2 tablespoons olive oil
1 tablespoon raspberry vinegar or
   cider vinegar
1 teaspoon sugar
1/2 teaspoon salt
Pepper to taste
2 pints fresh strawberries

Serves 8

*B*lanch the peas in a saucepan of boiling salted water for 30 seconds; drain. Plunge the peas into a bowl of ice water to stop the cooking process. Drain the peas and dry well.

Process the olive oil, vinegar, sugar, 1/2 teaspoon salt, pepper and 4 or 5 strawberries in a blender until smooth. Remove any strings from the peas. Cut the peas into halves. Slice the remaining strawberries. Combine with the peas in a bowl. Add the dressing and toss to mix.

Note: Recipe compliments of Sarah Fritschner.

PLANTATION TEA

7 tea bags
12 stems of mint
1/2 to 1 cup sugar
4 cups boiling water
1 (6-ounce) can frozen lemonade concentrate
3 cups cold water
1 1/2 cups pineapple juice
Additional mint sprigs for garnish

Makes 2 quarts

*P*lace the tea bags, mint stems and sugar in a heatproof pitcher. Add the boiling water and stir until the sugar is dissolved. Let stand for 30 minutes. Remove the tea bags and mint, squeezing the liquid out of the tea bags and mint. Discard the tea bags and mint.

Stir in the lemonade, cold water and pineapple juice. Chill until ready to serve. Pour into glasses filled with crushed ice and garnish with mint sprigs.

Note: This recipe was originally featured in *CORDONBLUEGRASS*, the Junior League of Louisville's second cookbook.

COCONUT CREAM PIE

1 1/2 tablespoons cornstarch
1 1/2 tablespoons all-purpose flour
3/4 cup sugar
Pinch of salt
2 cups milk, at room temperature
3 jumbo egg yolks
1 tablespoon vanilla extract
1 cup sweetened shredded or flaked coconut
1 baked (9-inch) pie shell
6 jumbo egg whites
3/4 cup sugar
1 tablespoon sweetened shredded or
   flaked coconut

Serves 8

Mix the cornstarch, flour, 3/4 cup sugar and the salt in a saucepan. Whisk in the milk and egg yolks. Cook until thick, stirring constantly. Stir in the vanilla and 1 cup coconut. Pour into the pie shell.

Beat the egg whites in a mixing bowl until foamy. Beat in 3/4 cup sugar gradually until the sugar is dissolved and stiff peaks form. Spread over the filling, sealing to the edge. Sprinkle with 1 tablespoon coconut.

Bake in a preheated 350-degree oven for 11 minutes or until light brown. Remove to a wire rack to cool.

Note: When making meringue, a general rule of thumb is to add 2 tablespoons of sugar per egg white. To help prevent the meringue from separating from the pie, spread the meringue over piping hot filling and make sure to smooth it all the way to the edge.

TEA IT UP

1 ounce Larceny Bourbon
1 ounce PAMA Pomegranate Liqueur
3 ounces iced tea
3 ounces lemonade
Dash of peach bitters
Lemon slice and mint sprig for garnish

Serves 1

Combine the bourbon, liqueur, tea, lemonade and bitters in a mason jar. Fill with ice. Garnish with a lemon wheel and mint sprig.

Lilies for the Fillies Cocktail Party

Serves 8 to 12

PULLED PORK CORN POPPERS

KENTUCKY COUNTRY HAM TORTE

CALL TO POST ASPARAGUS SALAD

AUNT SALLY'S PICKLES

DOWN THE STRETCH SHRIMP AND GRITS

ROASTED BUTTERFLIED LEG OF LAMB WITH MINT PEPPER JELLY

POMEGRANATE SALMON

BOURBON BALLS

KENTUCKY TIRAMISU

TRIPLE CROWN PIE SHOOTERS

BLUSHING LADY

OAKS LILY

Lilies for the Fillies Cocktail Party Menu Sponsored by

Churchill Downs

CHURCHILL DOWNS

Triple Crown Pie Shooters

PULLED PORK CORN POPPERS

PORK

1 (2 1/2-pound) pork shoulder
3 cups cider vinegar
2 tablespoons brown sugar
1 1/2 teaspoons ground cumin
1 1/2 teaspoons red pepper flakes
1 1/2 teaspoons chili powder
1 teaspoon kosher salt
1/2 onion, chopped
1/2 cup cola
Tortilla chips
6 ounces goat cheese, crumbled (optional)

Makes 25 to 50

*P*lace the pork fat side down in a roasting pan and pour the vinegar over the top. Sprinkle with the brown sugar, cumin, red pepper flakes, chili powder, salt and onion.

Bake, covered, in a preheated 300-degree oven for 4 hours. Remove the pork to a work surface and let cool. Strain the pan drippings into a saucepan. Simmer over medium heat until reduced by half. Stir in the cola and simmer for 2 minutes.

Shred the pork from the bone and place in a bowl. Add the cola sauce and mix well. Chill until ready to serve. To serve, spoon the pork onto tortilla chips. Top with the mango salsa and sprinkle with the goat cheese.

MANGO SALSA

3/4 cup chopped mango
3/4 cup finely chopped avocado
1/4 cup chopped jalapeño chile
1/4 cup lime juice
1/2 cup chopped cilantro
1 red onion, chopped (optional)

Makes 2 1/2 cups

*C*ombine the mango, avocado, jalapeño chile, lime juice, cilantro and onion in a bowl and mix well.

Chef: Chef Kathy Cary, Lilly's—
A Kentucky Bistro

BLUSHING LADY

1 ounce PAMA Pomegranate Liqueur
2 ounces Burnett's Vodka
1 ounce pink grapefruit juice
Superfine sugar

Serves 1

*C*ombine the liqueur, vodka, and grapefruit juice in a shaker over ice. Shake vigorously for 30 seconds. Strain into a chilled martini glass rimmed with sugar.

Kentucky Country Ham Torte

1 tablespoon unsalted butter, melted
3 cups finely ground unsalted saltine crackers
3/4 cup (3 ounces) grated Parmesan cheese
6 tablespoons unsalted butter, melted
32 ounces cream cheese, softened
7 eggs
2 cups (8 ounces) shredded Gruyère cheese
1 1/2 cups (6 to 8 ounces) chopped good-quality
  country ham
1/2 cup finely chopped chives
2 teaspoons white pepper

Serves 20

Brush a 9-inch springform pan with 1 tablespoon melted butter. Combine the crackers, Parmesan cheese and 6 tablespoons melted butter in a bowl and mix well. Reserve 1/2 cup of the crumb mixture. Press the remaining crumb mixture over the bottom and up the side of the springform pan. Chill until ready to fill.

Beat the cream cheese and eggs in a mixing bowl until smooth. Beat in the Gruyère cheese, ham, chives and white pepper. Pour into the crust and sprinkle with the reserved crumb mixture. Place on a rimmed baking sheet. Bake in a preheated 300-degree oven for 1 hour or until the center is set.

Cool on a wire rack for 30 minutes. Loosen the side of the pan with a sharp knife and remove. Serve warm or at room temperature with water crackers. This can be made 1 day ahead and chilled, covered. Allow to stand at room temperature for 2 hours before serving.

Decked out in pink, thousands of attendees, male and female, gather at Churchill Downs to celebrate cancer survivors during the Kentucky Oaks. Since 2009 the track has donated a portion of its proceeds to charities focused on finding a cure. The Junior League of Louisville is also a proponent of raising awareness by providing outreach and support through its Keep In Touch Breast Cancer Project. With support from the Louisville Affiliate of Susan G. Komen for the Cure, the Junior League of Louisville started Living Pink—a series of educational seminars focused on improving the quality of life and self-esteem of survivors and newly diagnosed individuals. Show your support by hosting a "pink" cocktail party on Oaks night.

CALL TO POST ASPARAGUS SALAD

1/4 cup white wine vinegar
2 tablespoons Dijon mustard
1 tablespoon minced shallot
3/4 teaspoon salt
3/4 teaspoon pepper
1/3 cup vegetable oil
2 tablespoons walnut oil or olive oil
2 bunches asparagus
1/4 cup walnuts, toasted and chopped
    for garnish
2 tablespoons chopped fresh parsley
    for garnish

Serves 8 to 10

Whisk the vinegar, Dijon mustard, shallot, salt and pepper in a bowl. Add the vegetable oil in a thin stream, whisking constantly. Whisk in the walnut oil.

Snap off the woody ends of the asparagus. Steam the asparagus over a saucepan of simmering water until tender-crisp. Plunge the asparagus into a bowl of ice water to stop the cooking process; drain.

Arrange the asparagus on a platter and drizzle with the dressing. Garnish with the walnuts and parsley.

Note: To toast nuts, arrange the nuts in a single layer in a skillet. Cook over medium-high heat for 5 minutes or until fragrant, stirring or shaking the pan constantly.

AUNT SALLY'S PICKLES

1 (1-gallon) jar whole dill pickles
5 cups sugar
1 garlic bulb, chopped
1/4 cup Tabasco sauce

Makes 8 to 10 pints

Drain the pickles, reserving the juice. Cut the pickles into 1/2-inch slices. Layer one-fifth of the pickles in the bottom of the pickle jar. Sprinkle with 1 cup sugar, one-fifth of the garlic and one-fifth of the Tabasco sauce.

Continue the layering process with the remaining ingredients. Fill the jar with the reserved pickle juice. Seal the jar and invert. Let stand at room temperature for 5 days, shaking the jar each day. Pack the pickles into hot sterilized 1-pint jars and fill with the liquid. Seal with 2-piece lids. Store in the refrigerator.

Note: This recipe was originally featured in the Junior League of Louisville's Tabasco award-winning third cookbook, *Splendor in the Bluegrass*.

DOWN THE STRETCH SHRIMP AND GRITS

CHEESE GRITS

4 cups chicken broth
4 cups water
2 tablespoons butter
Salt to taste
2 cups quick-cooking grits
1/4 teaspoon garlic powder
16 ounces shredded white Cheddar cheese
1/2 cup cream
2 tablespoons butter
1/2 teaspoon hot red pepper sauce
White pepper to taste

Serves 8 to 12

SHRIMP

2 pounds uncooked jumbo shrimp,
    peeled and deveined
1/2 teaspoon cayenne pepper
1 pound bacon
16 ounces shiitake mushrooms, sliced
4 garlic cloves, finely chopped
1 cup good-quality white wine
Salt and black pepper to taste
1 bunch scallions, chopped

Serves 8 to 12

Bring the broth, water, 2 tablespoons butter and salt to a boil in a saucepan over medium-high heat. Whisk in the grits and garlic powder gradually. Reduce the heat to medium and cook for 8 minutes or until the grits are thick, stirring occasionally.

Whisk in the cheese a small amount at a time until melted. Stir in the cream and 2 tablespoons butter. Stir in the hot sauce and white pepper. Keep warm until ready to serve.

Note: You may substitute water for the chicken broth.

Sprinkle the shrimp with the cayenne pepper. Cook the bacon in a skillet until crisp; drain, reserving 2 tablespoons of the drippings in the skillet. Crumble the bacon.

Add the mushrooms to the reserved drippings and sauté for 7 minutes. Add the garlic and sauté for 2 minutes. Stir in the wine and shrimp. Cook until the shrimp turn pink, stirring constantly. Season with salt and black pepper.

Spoon equal portions of the cheese grits into martini glasses and top with the shrimp mixture. Sprinkle with the scallions and crumbled bacon.

ROASTED BUTTERFLIED LEG OF LAMB

1 (5-pound) boneless butterflied leg of lamb
12 garlic cloves
1/4 cup chopped fresh rosemary
1/2 cup olive oil
1/2 cup marsala or dry red wine
1 tablespoon salt
1 tablespoon pepper
6 garlic cloves, minced
1/4 cup chopped fresh mint
1 tablespoon chopped fresh oregano
Mint Pepper Jelly (below)

Serves 16 to 24

*C*ut twelve small slits into the fatty side of the lamb. Insert one garlic clove and an equal portion of the rosemary into each slit. Place the lamb in a large dish. Whisk the olive oil, wine, salt, pepper, minced garlic, mint and oregano in a bowl. Pour over the lamb and turn to coat. Marinate at room temperature for 1 hour or covered in the refrigerator for 12 hours or longer, turning occasionally to coat.

To grill: Remove the lamb to a preheated grill, reserving the marinade. Grill for 10 to 12 minutes or until well charred, basting several times with the marinade. Turn over the lamb. Grill for 10 to 12 minutes or until well charred and to 130 degrees on a meat thermometer for medium-rare, basting several times with the marinade.

Remove the lamb to a cutting board and let stand for 15 minutes before slicing. Discard any remaining marinade. Serve with Mint Pepper Jelly and crusty French bread.

To roast: Remove the lamb to a large roasting pan, reserving the marinade. Roast in a preheated 425-degree oven for 20 minutes. Reduce the heat to 350 degrees and baste the lamb with the reserved marinade. Roast for 1 1/4 hours or to 135 degrees on a meat thermometer, basting every 20 to 30 minutes with the marinade. Remove the lamb to a cutting board and let stand for 15 minutes before slicing. Discard any remaining marinade. Serve with Mint Pepper Jelly and crusty French bread.

MINT PEPPER JELLY

1 small jar hot pepper jelly
3 tablespoons red wine vinegar
1/4 cup chopped fresh mint
1 teaspoon chopped fresh oregano
Salt and pepper to taste

Serves 16 to 24

*W*hisk the jelly, vinegar, mint, oregano, salt and pepper in a bowl. Spoon into an airtight container and refrigerate for up to 1 week.

POMEGRANATE SALMON

2 cups ketchup
2/3 cup PAMA Pomegranate Liqueur
5 tablespoons pomegranate molasses
1/4 cup cranberry juice
1/2 cup packed brown sugar
1 teaspoon minced garlic
1 tablespoon cider vinegar
1 tablespoon Worcestershire sauce
1/8 teaspoon cayenne pepper
Olive oil
1 (2 1/2- to 3-pound) salmon fillet,
    about 1-inch thick
Salt and black pepper to taste

Serves 6

Pick up some "New American Lamb" produced by Four Hills Farm in Salvisa, Kentucky, to make the Roasted Butterflied Leg of Lamb recipe (page 44). The vegetation-fed Katahdin lambs that are raised on this farm shed their winter coat naturally, creating a milder flavor due to the lack of lanolin production from wool. This quality lamb can be found at Marksbury Farm Market in Lancaster, Kentucky; Whole Foods; and Fishmarket, Inc., in Louisville.

Mix the ketchup, pomegranate liqueur, pomegranate molasses, cranberry juice, brown sugar, garlic, vinegar, Worcestershire sauce and cayenne pepper in a saucepan. Cook over medium heat until the sugar dissolves, stirring constantly. Bring to a boil, then reduce the heat. Simmer for 20 minutes, stirring frequently. Remove from the heat and cool completely.

Remove enough sauce to coat the salmon to a separate bowl. Preheat the grill or broiler. Brush the grill rack with olive oil if grilling. Brush the flesh side of the salmon with olive oil and sprinkle with salt and black pepper.

Place the salmon skin side down on the grill rack or broiler pan. Grill or broil 4 inches from the heat source for 5 minutes. Brush with the sauce in the bowl. Discard any sauce remaining in the bowl. Cook the salmon for 2 to 3 minutes longer or until the fish begins to flake.

Remove to a cutting board and cut into servings. Drizzle each serving with 1 to 2 tablespoons of the remaining sauce. Refrigerate remaining sauce for another use.

Note: Recipe compliments of Heaven Hill Distilleries, Inc.

BOURBON BALLS

1 cup pecans, finely chopped
1/3 cup Kentucky bourbon
1/2 cup (1 stick) unsalted butter, softened
1 (1-pound) package confectioners' sugar
2 cups (12 ounces) chocolate chips
4 ounces paraffin, grated
48 pecan halves, toasted

Makes 4 dozen

Combine the chopped pecans and bourbon in a bowl. Let stand, covered, for several hours to overnight. Beat the butter and confectioners' sugar in a bowl. Add the pecan mixture and mix well. Chill, covered, for 1 hour. Shape into 48 balls and arrange on a plate. Chill for 3 hours or freeze for 30 minutes.

Melt the chocolate chips and paraffin in the top of a double boiler over simmering water, stirring frequently. Line a rimmed baking sheet with waxed paper. Using a wooden skewer, dip each bourbon ball in the chocolate mixture to coat. Shake off any excess chocolate and place on the waxed paper.

Fill the holes in the bourbon balls with a small amount of melted chocolate; top each with a pecan half. Chill until firm. Store in an airtight container in the refrigerator for 1 to 2 days to allow the flavors to develop. Bring to room temperature before serving.

Note: You may roll the bourbon balls in confectioners' sugar, granulated sugar, baking cocoa or chopped nuts instead of coating in melted chocolate.

KENTUCKY TIRAMISU

8 ounces mascarpone cheese, softened
3/4 cup heavy whipping cream
1/3 cup good-quality Kentucky bourbon
2/3 cup confectioners' sugar
1 angel food cake, cut into slices
1/3 cup brewed espresso, chilled
2 quarts fresh strawberries, thinly sliced
1 cup heavy whipping cream
2 tablespoons granulated sugar
3 ounces semisweet chocolate
Mint leaves for garnish

Serves 12

Beat the mascarpone cheese, 3/4 cup cream, the bourbon and confectioners' sugar in a mixing bowl until medium peaks form. Brush the cake slices with the espresso and then cut into cubes. Layer the cake cubes, cheese mixture and strawberries one-half at a time in a 3-quart glass trifle bowl. Chill, covered, for 2 hours.

Beat 1 cup cream in a mixing bowl until almost stiff. Add the granulated sugar and beat until stiff peaks form. Shave the chocolate into long curls with a vegetable peeler. Top each serving of tiramisu with a dollop of whipped cream and chocolate curls and garnish with mint leaves.

TRIPLE CROWN PIE SHOOTERS

1 cup sugar
1/2 cup all-purpose flour
1 tablespoon cornstarch
2 eggs, lightly beaten
1/2 cup (1 stick) salted butter,
   melted and cooled
2 tablespoons Kentucky bourbon or water
1 tablespoon vanilla extract
1 cup shortbread cookies, crumbled
1 cup pecans, finely chopped
1 cup (6 ounces) mini chocolate chips
1 (7-ounce) can refrigerated whipped cream
Additional finely chopped pecans and
   miniture chocolate chips for garnish

Serves 24

Whisk the sugar, flour and cornstarch in a bowl. Whisk in the eggs, butter, bourbon and vanilla until smooth. Pour into a saucepan or skillet. Cook until slightly thickened, stirring frequently. Remove from the heat and cool slightly. (If batter cools completely or becomes too thick, cook over low heat, adding 1 teaspoon of water at a time and stirring until the mixture warms and thins.)

Layer 2 teaspoons of the crumbled cookies, 1 teaspoon of the pecans and 1 teaspoon of the chocolate chips in each of 24 (2-ounce) shot glasses. Top each with 2 teaspoons of the custard, 1 teaspoon of the pecans and 1 teaspoon of the chocolate chips. Top each with a dollop of whipped cream. Garnish with additional pecans and chocolate chips.

Arrange the shooters on a serving tray and insert a miniature tasting spoon into each shooter.

Note: Disposable shot glasses can be found at most party supply stores.

OAKS LILY

1 ounce vodka
1 ounce sweet-and-sour mix
3 ounces cranberry juice
Splash of Triple Sec
Orange wedge and maraschino cherry
   for garnish

Serves 1

Combine the vodka, sweet-and-sour mix, cranberry juice and liqueur in a cocktail shaker. Shake or stir to mix. Pour over crushed ice in a tall glass. Add a straw and garnish with an orange wedge and cherry.

Note: This is the official drink of the Kentucky Oaks.

Run for the Roses Brunch

Serves 8

AND THEY'RE OFF AMARETTO FRUIT SALAD

BIBB LETTUCE WITH BENEDICTINE DRESSING

MINIATURE HOT BROWN APPETIZERS WITH MORNAY SAUCE

PIMENTO CHEESE–STUFFED MUSHROOMS

FAST TRACK FRITTATA

WINNER'S CIRCLE CORN PUDDING

SOUTHERN COUNTRY HAM AND CHIVE BISCUITS

BOURBON BANANA BREAD WITH STRAWBERRY COMPOTE

MINT JULEP CAKE

CLASSIC MINT JULEP

Run for the Roses Brunch Menu Sponsored by

North End Cafe

Fast Track Frittata

AND THEY'RE OFF AMARETTO FRUIT SALAD

1 bunch seedless grapes
1 small honeydew melon, chopped
1 small pineapple, chopped
1 pint strawberries, chopped
1/2 cup amaretto
1/2 cup white wine
2 teaspoons fresh lemon juice
3 tablespoons sugar
1 large banana
1 mint sprig for garnish

Serves 8

Cut the grapes into halves. Combine with the melon, pineapple and strawberries in a bowl. Whisk the amaretto, wine, lemon juice and sugar in a bowl until the sugar is dissolved. Pour over the fruit and stir gently to mix. Chill, covered, for 8 to 10 hours. Slice the banana and add to the salad. Stir gently to mix. Garnish with the mint and serve immediately.

Variation: Any seasonal fruit may be substituted in this salad.

Commonly referred to as "the most exciting two minutes in sports," the Kentucky Derby is the most historic and well recognized thoroughbred horse race in the world. The 1¼-mile run for three-year-olds takes place on the first Saturday in May at the infamous Churchill Downs racetrack. Known for a rich tradition of mint juleps and stylish hats, the Kentucky Derby draws an average of 150,000 attendees each year comprised of local residents, celebrities, and royalty. Whether or not you are attending the Derby, invite your friends over for brunch to kick off the best day of the year.

BIBB LETTUCE WITH BENEDICTINE DRESSING

BIBB SALAD

8 slices medium-thick pancetta, crisp-cooked
   and crumbled
2 heads Bibb lettuce, chopped, preferably
   Grateful Greens lettuce
1 cup grape tomatoes or cherry
   tomatoes, halved

BENEDICTINE DRESSING

1 small seedless cucumber, peeled
1/2 cup sour cream
1/4 cup buttermilk
1 tablespoon chopped fresh dill weed
2 green onions, chopped
1 teaspoon lemon juice
Dash of hot red pepper sauce
Salt and freshly ground pepper to taste

Serves 8

Combine the pancetta, lettuce and tomatoes in a bowl and toss to mix. Drizzle with the Benedictine dressing and toss lightly to coat.

Shred the cucumber and drain on paper towels. Process the cucumber, sour cream, buttermilk, dill weed, green onions, lemon juice, hot sauce, salt and pepper in a blender until smooth. Chill until ready to serve.

Grateful Greens is a hydroponic lettuce and herb farm located in Clarksville, Indiana, just 5 minutes north of downtown Louisville. Their Bibb lettuce is the perfect pairing to the Benedictine Salad Dressing and can be found in many local specialty food shops.

MINIATURE HOT BROWN APPETIZERS WITH MORNAY SAUCE

MINIATURE HOT BROWNS

1 cup finely chopped roasted turkey breast
1/2 cup chopped tomato
24 miniature tart shells
2 slices bacon, crisp-cooked and crumbled
1/2 cup (2 ounces) grated Romano cheese
2 teaspoons paprika
2 teaspoons chopped parsley

Serves 24

Combine the turkey, tomato and 1 cup Mornay Sauce in a bowl and mix well. Spoon into a pastry bag fitted with a large tip. Arrange the tart shells 1/2 inch apart on a parchment-covered baking sheet. Fill each tart shell with an equal portion of the turkey mixture. Sprinkle the tarts with equal portions of the bacon, cheese and paprika.

Bake in a preheated 325-degree oven for 8 to 10 minutes or until the tarts are heated through. Sprinkle the tarts with equal portions of the parsley and serve warm.

MORNAY SAUCE

1/4 cup (1/2 stick) butter
3 tablespoons all-purpose flour
11/2 cups milk
6 tablespoons grated Parmesan cheese
1 egg
1/4 cup whipped cream (optional)
1/4 teaspoon salt
1/4 teaspoon white pepper
2 dashes of hot red pepper sauce

Makes 2 cups

Melt the butter in a saucepan. Whisk in the flour gradually. Cook for 3 minutes, whisking constantly; do not let brown. Whisk in the milk gradually. Cook until the sauce thickens, whisking constantly; do not let boil. Add the cheese and cook until the cheese is melted, stirring constantly.

Beat the egg in a small bowl. Stir in 1/2 cup of the hot sauce slowly, stirring constantly. Add the egg mixture to the saucepan and mix well. Remove from the heat and fold in the whipped cream. Stir in the salt, white pepper and hot sauce. Store any leftover sauce in the refrigerator.

Chef: Chef Laurent Géroli, The Brown Hotel

PIMENTO CHEESE–STUFFED MUSHROOMS

PIMENTO CHEESE

4 ounces cream cheese, softened
1 red bell pepper, finely chopped
1/4 teaspoon cayenne pepper
1 tablespoon Dijon mustard
1/4 cup Durkee sauce
1/3 cup chopped fresh parsley
2 tablespoons mayonnaise
2 tablespoons orange liqueur
16 ounces Cheddar cheese, shredded

STUFFED MUSHROOMS

32 ounces baby portobello mushrooms
4 slices bacon, crisp-cooked and crumbled
1/2 cup strawberry preserves (optional)
2 tablespoons hot water (optional)

Makes 48

*P*rocess the cream cheese, bell pepper, cayenne pepper, Dijon mustard, Durkee sauce, parsley, mayonnaise and liqueur in a food processor until well mixed. Remove to a bowl. Fold the Cheddar cheese into the cream cheese mixture. Chill until ready to use.

*F*ill the mushrooms with equal portions of the pimento cheese and arrange in a baking dish. Bake in a preheated 350-degree oven for 25 to 30 minutes or until the mushrooms are tender.

Sprinkle the mushrooms with the bacon and bake for 2 minutes longer. Mix the strawberry preserves with the water in a small bowl. Drizzle over the mushrooms and serve.

CLASSIC MINT JULEP

2 ounces Evan Williams Single Barrel Bourbon
2 or 3 mint sprigs
1 teaspoon sugar
1/2 teaspoon water
Additional mint sprig for garnish

Serves 1

*P*our the bourbon in a cup 3/4 full of shaved ice. Bruise 2 or 3 mint sprigs with your fingers and rub over the rim of the cup. Dissolve the sugar in the water in a small bowl. Stir the sugar solution gently into the bourbon. Add enough additional shaved ice to fill the cup. Garnish with an additional mint sprig.

FAST TRACK FRITTATA

1 large Roma tomato
2 tablespoons butter
1 cup thinly sliced leeks, white and light
　　green parts
2 1/2 cups bite-size asparagus pieces
Salt and black pepper to taste
8 eggs
1/2 cup (2 ounces) shredded Swiss cheese
1/4 cup chopped fresh basil
1/4 teaspoon salt
1 teaspoon nutmeg
1/2 teaspoon white pepper
1/4 cup (1 ounce) shredded Swiss cheese
1 tablespoon chopped fresh basil

Serves 8

*C*ut the tomato into 1/4-inch slices and lay on paper towels to drain. Melt the butter in a 10-inch nonstick broilerproof skillet over medium heat. Add the leeks and sauté for 4 minutes. Add the asparagus and season with salt to taste and black pepper. Sauté for 6 minutes or until the vegetables are tender.

Whisk the eggs in a bowl. Fold in 1/2 cup cheese, 1/4 cup basil, 1/4 teaspoon salt, the nutmeg and white pepper. Add to the skillet and fold the vegetables into the eggs. Cook for 5 to 7 minutes or until almost set. Top with the tomato slices and sprinkle with 1/4 cup cheese.

Place the skillet under a preheated 500-degree broiler. Broil for 4 minutes or until golden brown and the eggs are puffed and set. Sprinkle with 1 tablespoon basil. Cut into wedges and serve.

WINNER'S CIRCLE CORN PUDDING

2 (15-ounce) cans cream-style corn
2/3 cup sugar
1/4 cup all-purpose flour
1 cup milk
2 dashes of nutmeg
2 eggs
1 teaspoon salt
1/4 teaspoon pepper
1/4 cup (1/2 stick) butter, melted

Serves 8

*C*ombine the corn, sugar, flour, milk, nutmeg, eggs, salt and pepper in a bowl and mix well. Pour into a greased 8×8-inch baking dish. Drizzle the melted butter over the top. Bake in a preheated 325-degree oven for 1 1/4 hours or until a wooden pick inserted in the center comes out clean.

SOUTHERN COUNTRY HAM AND CHIVE BISCUITS

1 teaspoon unsalted butter
4 slices country ham, chopped
8 ounces cream cheese, softened
2/3 cup unsalted butter, softened
1 1/3 cups self-rising flour
2 tablespoons chopped chives
Additional melted butter

Makes 3 dozen

Melt 1 teaspoon butter in a skillet. Add the ham and sauté until golden brown. Remove the ham to paper towels to drain. Pulse the cream cheese, 2/3 cup butter and the flour in a food processor to form a ball. Add the ham and chives and pulse until combined.

Divide the dough into two balls. Flatten each ball and wrap in waxed paper or plastic wrap. Chill for at least 30 minutes. Roll out each ball of dough on a floured surface to 1/4 inch and fold in half to make 1/2-inch thickness. Cut with a 1- to 1 1/4-inch biscuit cutter. Arrange the biscuits 1 inch apart on an ungreased baking sheet. Chill for 10 to 20 minutes or until cold.

Bake on the top rack in a preheated 425-degree oven for 12 to 15 minutes, rotating the baking sheets halfway through the baking process. Remove the biscuits to a wire rack to cool. Brush lightly with additional melted butter before serving.

If you find yourself near the middle of Western Kentucky, make time to stop by Newsom's Old Mill Store to pick up Col. Bill Newsom's Aged Kentucky Country Ham. It's the only place, other than their website, that this mouthwatering ham can be purchased. A whole ham will keep indefinitely if hung in a cool, dry place. Keep some on hand and wait for the perfect occasion to make the best Southern Country Ham and Chive Biscuit you'll find in all fifty states.

BOURBON BANANA BREAD WITH STRAWBERRY COMPOTE

BOURBON BANANA BREAD

1/4 cup good-quality Kentucky bourbon
1/2 cup chopped pecans
1 1/3 cups all-purpose flour
3/4 teaspoon salt
1/2 teaspoon baking soda
1/4 teaspoon baking powder
5 1/3 tablespoons unsalted butter, softened
2/3 cup granulated sugar
2 eggs, lightly beaten
1 teaspoon vanilla extract
2 teaspoons good-quality Kentucky bourbon
1 cup mashed very ripe bananas
    (about 2 bananas)
8 ounces mascarpone cheese, softened
1 cup confectioners' sugar, sifted

Serves 8

*P*our 1/4 cup bourbon over the pecans in a bowl. Chill for 24 hours. Mix the flour, salt, baking soda and baking powder together. Beat the butter and granulated sugar in a mixing bowl on high speed for 2 to 3 minutes. Add the dry ingredients and beat to the consistency of brown sugar. Beat in the eggs, vanilla and 2 teaspoons bourbon gradually. Fold in the banana and pecan mixture. Pour into a greased 4×8-inch loaf pan and smooth the top.

Bake in a preheated 350-degree oven for 50 to 60 minutes or until a wooden pick inserted in the center comes out clean. Cool in the pan for 5 to 10 minutes. Remove to a wire rack to cool completely. Slice the banana bread. Serve each slice with a dollop of cheese and top with Strawberry Compote. Dust with the confectioners' sugar.

Note: Plain or vanilla Greek yogurt may be substituted for the mascarpone cheese.

STRAWBERRY COMPOTE

1/2 cup packed brown sugar
Grated zest of 1 orange
Juice of 2 oranges
1 cinnamon stick
2 1/2 cups strawberries, thickly sliced

Makes 2 cups

*B*ring the brown sugar, orange zest, orange juice and cinnamon stick to a boil in a saucepan. Stir in the strawberries and return to a boil. Remove from the heat and remove the cinnamon stick. Pour the compote into a heatproof bowl and let cool.

MINT JULEP CAKE

CAKE

3 cups cake flour
1 teaspoon salt
1 teaspoon baking powder
$^1/_2$ teaspoon baking soda
2 cups sugar
1 cup (2 sticks) butter, softened
4 eggs
2 teaspoons vanilla extract
1 cup buttermilk
$^1/_2$ cup sugar
$^1/_2$ cup (1 stick) butter, softened
$^1/_2$ cup Kentucky bourbon
Mint leaves for garnish

Serves 12 to 18

Mix the flour, salt, baking powder and baking soda together. Beat 2 cups sugar and 1 cup butter in a mixing bowl until light and fluffy. Add the eggs one at a time, beating well after each addition. Beat in the vanilla. Add the dry ingredients and buttermilk alternately, stirring just until combined after each addition.

Pour into a 10-inch bundt pan coated with nonstick cooking spray and smooth the top. Bake in a preheated 325-degree oven for 45 to 50 minutes or until a wooden pick inserted in the center comes out clean. Remove to a wire rack.

Heat $^1/_2$ cup sugar, $^1/_2$ cup butter and the bourbon in a saucepan until the butter is melted, stirring constantly. Poke holes in the top of the cake with a skewer. Pour the bourbon sauce evenly over the hot cake. Let cool completely. Invert the cake onto a serving plate. Drizzle the mint glaze over the cake and garnish the center of the cake with mint leaves.

MINT GLAZE

$1^1/_2$ cups confectioners' sugar
1 tablespoon (or more) milk
1 tablespoon clear crème de menthe

Makes $^3/_4$ cup

Whisk the confectioners' sugar, milk and crème de menthe in a bowl until smooth. Whisk in additional milk if the glaze is too thick to drizzle.

Summer

Poplar Terrace

Summer

Poplar Terrace, home of Junior League of Louisville Sustainer Christina Lee Brown and her late husband, philanthropist Owsley Brown II, overlooks the scenic banks of the Ohio River. Constructed in 1911, the home exudes the best of southern hospitality as well as fine Kentucky bourbon, which flows from a handcrafted mint julep fountain. You, too, can celebrate the tradition of the Bluegrass at your next gathering by displaying a fresh bouquet of vibrant flowers on a crisp, white tablecloth. Serving drinks in frosted mint julep cups sets the mood for an elegant summer luncheon or Sunday brunch.

SUMMER MENUS

Summer Chapter Sponsored by

LAUREN ADAMS OGDEN

Patio Wine Party

Serves 6

FULL-BODIED EDAMAME DIP WITH SPICED PITA CHIPS

SPICY ROASTED SHRIMP COCKTAIL AND SAUCE

ADOBO-RUBBED PORK TENDERLOIN WITH
CHIPOTLE-ORANGE SAUCE AND SWEET CORN GRIT CAKES

PERFECT BLEND AVOCADO TOMATO STACKS

PROSCIUTTO WITH MELON AND ASPARAGUS

SWEET FINISH SORBET TRIO

SANGRIA BLANCA

Patio Wine Party Menu Sponsored by

Colonial Designs

Colonial Designs
of St. Matthews

Spicy Roasted Shrimp Cocktail and Sauce

FULL-BODIED EDAMAME DIP WITH SPICED PITA CHIPS

EDAMAME DIP

5 large garlic cloves, peeled
1 teaspoon olive oil
2 cups edamame, shelled and cooked
1/2 cup ricotta cheese
1/4 cup fresh basil, chopped
2 tablespoons lemon juice
2 tablespoons freshly grated Parmesan cheese
1/4 cup olive oil
1/2 teaspoon grated lemon zest
1 teaspoon kosher salt
1/2 teaspoon freshly ground pepper

Serves 6 to 8

SPICED PITA CHIPS

1/4 cup olive oil
2 teaspoons ground cumin
1 teaspoon ground coriander
1/4 teaspoon cayenne pepper
2 teaspoons garlic salt
1/2 teaspoon black pepper
1 teaspoon onion powder
6 plain or whole wheat pita breads,
   each cut into 8 wedges

Makes 4 dozen pita chips

*P*lace the garlic on a sheet of foil. Drizzle with 1 teaspoon olive oil and seal the foil. Bake in a preheated 425-degree oven for 20 minutes. Open the foil and cool for 5 minutes. Process the edamame in a food processor for 30 seconds or until smooth. Add the garlic, ricotta cheese, basil, lemon juice and Parmesan cheese and pulse to mix. Add 1/4 cup olive oil in a fine stream, processing constantly until smooth. Remove to a bowl and stir in the lemon zest, salt and pepper. Serve with spiced pita chips.

*W*hisk the olive oil, cumin, coriander, cayenne pepper, garlic salt, black pepper and onion powder in a bowl. Add the pita wedges and toss to coat.

Spread the pita wedges in a single layer over two baking sheets. Bake in a preheated 375-degree oven for 15 minutes or until golden brown and crisp, tossing once during baking.

SPICY ROASTED SHRIMP COCKTAIL AND SAUCE

ROASTED SHRIMP

3 garlic cloves, minced
1 tablespoon minced shallot
2 pounds jumbo shrimp, peeled and
  deveined with tails
3 tablespoons olive oil
1 teaspoon salt
1/4 teaspoon pepper

Serves 4 to 6

COCKTAIL SAUCE

1/2 cup ketchup
1/2 cup chili sauce
1/4 cup grated sweet white onion
1/2 teaspoon finely chopped jalapeño
  chile or other hot chile
2 tablespoons horseradish
1 garlic clove, minced
1 teaspoon grated lemon zest
1 tablespoon fresh lemon juice
1/8 teaspoon salt

Makes 1 1/4 cup

Combine the garlic, shallot, shrimp, olive oil, salt and pepper in a bowl and toss to mix. Spread the shrimp in a single layer on a heavy rimmed baking sheet. Roast in a preheated 450-degree oven for 3 minutes. Turn the shrimp over and roast for 2 to 4 minutes longer or until the shrimp turn pink. Remove the shrimp to a shallow dish and partially cover. Chill for 2 hours. Serve with cocktail sauce.

Combine the ketchup, chili sauce, onion, jalapeño chile, horseradish, garlic, lemon zest, lemon juice and salt in a bowl and mix well. Chill, covered, for up to 24 hours.

Before it gets too hot to enjoy the outdoors, gather your friends and throw a dinner party and wine tasting on your patio or deck. Ask guests to bring a bottle of wine from their favorite local winery and have fun rating everyone's choices. With wineries throughout the Bluegrass State, you just might find a new favorite!

ADOBO-RUBBED PORK TENDERLOIN WITH CHIPOTLE-ORANGE SAUCE AND SWEET CORN GRIT CAKES

ADOBO-RUBBED PORK TENDERLOIN

1/2 cup olive oil
3 tablespoons chopped garlic
1 tablespoon cumin
1 tablespoon coriander
1 tablespoon kosher salt
1 tablespoon cayenne pepper
1 (2-pound) pork tenderloin, cut into
   equal portions

Combine the olive oil, garlic, cumin, coriander, salt and cayenne pepper in a bowl and mix well. Rub the mixture over the pork. Chill, covered, for at least 8 hours. Grill the pork over medium-hot coals to 160 degrees on a meat thermometer.

CHIPOTLE-ORANGE SAUCE

1/4 cup Kentucky bourbon
1 onion, chopped
1 tablespoon chopped garlic
3 ounces chipotle chiles in adobo sauce
1 cup crushed tomatoes
1 cup ketchup
1/2 cup rice wine vinegar
1/4 cup Worcestershire sauce
1 cup orange juice concentrate, thawed
1/4 cup honey
1 tablespoon paprika
1 tablespoon chili powder
1 teaspoon salt

Combine the bourbon, onion, garlic, chipotle chiles, tomatoes, ketchup, vinegar, Worcestershire sauce, orange juice concentrate, honey, paprika, chili powder and salt in a saucepan and mix well. Cook over medium-high heat for 5 minutes, stirring constantly. Strain through a medium mesh strainer into a bowl and discard the solids. Chill, covered, until ready to use.

Most people think of bourbon when they think Kentucky, but wineries in the Bluegrass are gaining speed. Skip a rock across the Ohio River to Southern Indiana and visit all nine wineries on the Uplands Wine Trail. For wine pairing suggestions, please turn to our guide on page 196.

SMOKED CHEDDAR CHIPOTLE SWEET CORN GRIT CAKES

3 cups water
1 tablespoon olive oil
1/4 teaspoon kosher salt
3/4 cup stone-ground grits
1/4 cup (1/2 stick) unsalted butter
1 1/2 tablespoons chipotle chiles in
   adobo sauce, chopped
8 ounces Cheddar cheese, cut into
   1-inch cubes
1/3 cup cooked fresh corn kernels
1 tablespoon olive oil
All-purpose flour
Additional olive oil
1/3 cup cooked fresh corn kernels for garnish
2 tablespoons chopped fresh cilantro

Serves 6

*W*ant a little cheese with your wine?
Stone Cross Farm and Cloverdale
Creamery say nothing comes close to
local cheese. Pair their Bellemoral Plain
with white wines; the Chive Onion
Bellemoral with a light red; the Smoked
Bellemoral with spicier wines like a
zinfandel, shiraz, or a pinot noir; and
the Cowbells in Clover with any quality
red wine.

*B*ring the water, 1 tablespoon olive oil and the salt to a boil in a saucepan. Stir in the grits and cook according to the package directions, stirring in the butter and chipotle chiles as the grits begin to thicken. Cook for 2 minutes longer. Stir in the cheese gradually. Cook until the cheese is melted, stirring constantly. Stir in 1/3 cup corn and remove from the heat.

Grease a 12×18-inch pan with 1 tablespoon olive oil. Spread the grits evenly into the pan. Press plastic wrap directly onto the grits and chill for 4 to 24 hours.

Cut the grits into squares or wedges and dust with flour. Heat a small amount of olive oil in a skillet. Add the cakes and fry for 2 minutes per side or until golden brown. Remove to a shallow baking pan. Bake in a preheated 350-degree oven for 3 to 5 minutes; keep warm.

Pour the chipotle-orange sauce into a saucepan and reheat over low heat. Place one grit cake in the center of each serving plate and arrange one piece of pork next to each grit cake. Spoon equal portions of the sauce around the grit cake and over the pork. Garnish with the corn and cilantro. Reserve any unused grit cakes for another purpose.

Chef: Chef Anthony Lamas, Seviche

PERFECT BLEND AVOCADO TOMATO STACKS

STACKS

6 heirloom tomatoes, sliced
Salt to taste
1/3 cup thinly sliced red onion
2 avocados, sliced
Coarsely ground pepper to taste (optional)

Serves 6

BUTTERMILK-CILANTRO DRESSING

1/3 cup low-fat buttermilk
1/4 cup chopped fresh cilantro
2 tablespoons sour cream
1 tablespoon mayonnaise
1/2 teaspoon grated lime zest
1/4 teaspoon minced fresh garlic
1/4 teaspoon salt
1/8 teaspoon ground cumin
1 dash of cayenne pepper

Makes 1/2 cup

*P*lace one tomato slice on each salad plate and sprinkle with salt. Top each tomato slice with a few onion slices and one avocado slice. Repeat the layers three more times, ending with avocado. Drizzle with the buttermilk-cilantro dressing and sprinkle with pepper.

*C*ombine the buttermilk, cilantro, sour cream, mayonnaise, lime zest, garlic, salt, cumin and cayenne pepper in a small food processor or blender. Process for 30 seconds or until puréed, stopping to scrape the side frequently. Pour into a bowl and chill, covered.

PROSCIUTTO WITH MELON AND ASPARAGUS

8 ounces asparagus spears
1 small cantaloupe
8 thin slices of prosciutto
6 ounces frisée salad mix
3/4 cup fresh raspberries
1 tablespoon freshly shaved Parmesan cheese

Serves 4 to 8

Trim the asparagus. Blanch in boiling water in a saucepan just until tender. Plunge into ice water to stop the cooking process. Drain again and set aside.

Cut the melon in half and remove the seeds. Cut each half into four equal wedges and cut away the rind. Separate the prosciutto slices and wrap around the melon slices.

Arrange the salad greens on a large serving platter. Top with the asparagus. Place the melon wedges on top of the asparagus. Scatter with the raspberries and Parmesan cheese. Drizzle the zesty vinaigrette over the top.

ZESTY VINAIGRETTE

1 tablespoon balsamic vinegar
1 tablespoon red wine vinegar
2 tablespoon orange juice
Dash of salt
Dash of pepper
1 tablespoon olive oil

Makes about 1/4 cup

Combine the balsamic vinegar, wine vinegar, olive oil, orange juice, salt and pepper in a bowl. Add the olive oil gradually, whisking constantly.

Sweet Finish Sorbet Trio

Blueberry-Lemon Sorbet

1¹/₂ cups sugar
1¹/₂ cups water
Zest of 1 large lemon
5 cups fresh blueberries
6 tablespoons water

Serves 8

Combine the sugar, 1¹/₂ cups water and the lemon zest in a saucepan. Cook over medium-low heat until the sugar is dissolved, stirring constantly.

Remove from the heat and cool completely. Remove and discard any large pieces of lemon zest. Purée the blueberries and 6 tablespoons water in a food processor. Pour through a fine mesh sieve over a bowl, pressing down on the pulp to remove all of the juice. Discard the pulp.

Mix 2 cups of the blueberry juice and 1¹/₄ cups of the lemon syrup in a bowl, reserving any unused blueberry juice for another purpose. Chill for at least 1 hour. Pour into an ice cream freezer container. Freeze using the manufacturer's directions. Remove to a sealable plastic container and freeze until ready to serve.

Wine Sorbet

1¹/₄ cups superfine sugar
1¹/₂ cups water
1 cup sweet white wine, such as
  ice wine or riesling
Juice of 2 large oranges
Juice of 4 large lemons

Serves 8

Combine the sugar, water and wine in a saucepan. Cook over medium heat until the sugar is dissolved, stirring constantly. Bring to a boil. Reduce the heat and simmer for 5 to 10 minutes or until the consistency of syrup. Remove from the heat and let cool for 1 hour. Remove to a chilled bowl and chill for 3 hours to overnight. Stir in the orange juice and lemon juice. Pour into an ice cream freezer container. Freeze using the manufacturer's directions. Remove to a sealable plastic container and freeze until ready to serve.

Raspberry Sorbet

1 cup sugar
1 1/2 cups water
1 cup Champagne
24 ounces raspberries

Serves 8

Variation: You may add up to 3 tablespoons of liqueur or other flavoring to the fruit purée.

*C*ombine the sugar, water and Champagne in a saucepan. Bring to a boil over medium heat, stirring constantly. Reduce the heat and simmer until the sugar is dissolved, stirring constantly. Remove from the heat and cool completely.

Purée the raspberries and half the cooled sugar syrup in a blender. Pour through a fine mesh sieve over a bowl, pressing down on the pulp to remove all of the juice. Discard the pulp and seeds. Mix the juice into the remaining sugar syrup and chill for 4 hours. Pour into an ice cream freezer container. Freeze using the manufacturer's directions. Remove to a sealable plastic container and freeze until ready to serve.

To serve: Place a small scoop of the Blueberry-Lemon sorbet in a dessert dish and top with a small scoop of the Wine Sorbet. Place a small scoop of Raspberry Sorbet on top. Garnish with a mint sprig and serve.

Sangria Blanca

1 (750-milliliter) bottle dry sparkling wine
1 1/2 cups white grape juice
1/2 cup orange liqueur
10 seedless green grapes, cut into halves
4 strawberries, sliced
1 peach, sliced
2 mint sprigs

Serves 8

*F*ill a large glass pitcher halfway with ice. Add the sparkling wine, grape juice, liqueur, grapes, strawberries, peach and mint and stir gently to mix. Serve chilled

On the Grill

Serves 8

HERB-STUFFED ARTICHOKES

GRILLED PEACH SALAD WITH SHAVED COUNTRY HAM AND SUMMER HERBS

BEST PIZZA DOUGH

CARAMELIZED ONION AND MUSHROOM PIZZA

TEQUILA-LIME CHICKEN AND SWEET CORN PIZZA

FIG-PROSCIUTTO PIZZA WITH ARUGULA

SWEET GRILLED FRUIT SKEWERS WITH HONEY YOGURT SAUCE

SKINNY AGAVE-RITA

On the Grill Menu Sponsored by

Maggie M. Heely, Event Warriors and Weekend Wedding Warrior, LLC

Fig-Prosciutto Pizza with Arugula

Herb-Stuffed Artichokes

4 large artichokes, washed and trimmed
1 teaspoon iodized salt
1 lemon, cut into halves
3 tablespoons olive oil
Grated zest and juice of 1 lemon
2 tablespoons olive oil
1/2 cup chopped pancetta or bacon
3 garlic cloves
1 cup bread crumbs
1/2 cup (2 ounces) grated Parmesan cheese
4 teaspoons chopped fresh oregano
4 teaspoons chopped fresh thyme
4 teaspoons chopped fresh basil
1/4 cup olive oil
1/4 cup white wine or water
Kosher salt or sea salt to taste
Pepper to taste
Additional olive oil (optional)

Serves 8

Remove the tough outer leaves from the artichokes. Cut the artichokes in half vertically and remove the fuzzy part above the heart. Fill a large saucepan with water and add 1 teaspoon salt. Squeeze the juice of 1 lemon into the water and add the lemon halves to the water. Add the artichokes, cover and bring to a boil. Turn off the heat and let stand, covered, for 5 to 7 minutes. Drain and pat the artichokes dry gently with paper towels. Arrange the artichokes cut side up in a baking pan. Drizzle with 3 tablespoons olive oil, the lemon zest and lemon juice. Chill, covered, for up to 24 hours.

Heat 2 tablespoons olive oil in a skillet. Add the pancetta and garlic and sauté until the pancetta is crispy; drain. Combine the pancetta mixture, bread crumbs, cheese, oregano, thyme, basil, 1/4 cup olive oil, the wine, kosher salt and pepper in a food processor and pulse to combine.

Grill the artichokes cut side down on a preheated grill over direct heat for 3 minutes. Turn the artichokes over and gently press equal portions of the stuffing into each cavity. Season with kosher salt and pepper. Grill over indirect heat for 20 minutes. Remove to a serving platter and drizzle with additional olive oil. Serve warm or at room temperature.

GRILLED PEACH SALAD WITH SHAVED COUNTRY HAM AND SUMMER HERBS

2 tablespoons extra-virgin olive oil
1 tablespoon balsamic vinegar
4 peaches, cut into halves
1 tablespoon extra-virgin olive oil
6 ounces country ham, chopped
1/4 cup fresh mint, chopped
1/4 cup fresh parsley, chopped
1/4 cup fresh basil, chopped
3 tablespoons extra-virgin olive oil
Juice of 1 lime
Kosher salt and freshly ground pepper
   to taste
8 cups baby spinach
1/2 cup crumbled goat cheese

Serves 6 to 8

Mix 2 tablespoons olive oil and the vinegar in a small bowl. Brush over the cut sides of the peach halves. Grill the peaches cut side down on a preheated grill over medium heat for 3 minutes or until grill marks appear and the skins start to loosen. Remove the peaches to a work surface and let cool until able to handle.

Remove the skins and chop the peaches into large chunks. Remove to a serving bowl and set aside.

Heat 1 tablespoon olive oil in a cast-iron skillet over medium-high heat until sizzling. Add the ham and sauté for 2 to 3 minutes or until crispy. Remove the ham to paper towels to drain.

Whisk the mint, parsley, basil, 3 tablespoons olive oil, the lime juice, salt and pepper in a bowl. Add the spinach, ham, cheese and dressing to taste to the peaches and toss to mix. Serve at room temperature.

Take a break from the stovetop and fire up the barbie—it's grillin' time! Tired of burgers and hotdogs on the Fourth of July? Switch things up with a pizza menu that doesn't require carryout or delivery. Let your kids help make the dough and top the pizzas and they'll be more likely to try creative toppings. Who knows, you may get away from ordering pepperoni pizzas forever!

BEST PIZZA DOUGH

1 envelope dry yeast
1 1/3 cups warm water
3 1/2 cups all-purpose flour
1 tablespoon salt
1 tablespoon sugar (optional)
2 tablespoons olive oil or nonstick
   cooking spray

Makes 2 (12-inch) pizza crusts

Combine the yeast and water in a small bowl. Let sit for 5 minutes. Combine with the flour, salt and sugar in a mixing bowl. Beat at low speed for 1 minute. Knead at medium speed for 10 minutes using a dough hook or knead on a floured surface until smooth and elastic. Coat a bowl with the olive oil. Add the dough, turning to coat. Let rise, covered with plastic wrap, in a warm place for 1 to 1 1/2 hours or until doubled in bulk. Punch down the dough and remove to a work surface. Divide into 2 balls and let rest for 10 minutes, loosely covered. Roll to 12-inch diameter circles on a lightly floured surface.

CARAMELIZED ONION AND MUSHROOM PIZZA

2 onions, thinly sliced crosswise
2 tablespoons olive oil
Salt and pepper to taste
1 tablespoon olive oil
8 ounces assorted wild mushrooms
   (such as cremini, oyster, chanterelle
   and shiitake), cut into bite-size pieces
6 garlic cloves, minced
1 cup dry white wine
1 tablespoon minced fresh thyme
Best Pizza Dough (above)
Truffle oil or olive oil
1 1/2 cups (6 ounces) shredded fontina cheese
1 tablespoon fresh thyme, minced

Makes 2 pizzas

Sauté the onions in 2 tablespoons olive oil in a skillet over medium heat for 20 minutes or until golden brown. Season with salt and pepper; remove from the heat. Sauté the mushrooms and garlic in 1 tablespoon olive oil in a skillet for several minutes. Stir in the wine. Simmer for 10 minutes or until the liquid is almost absorbed, stirring frequently. Stir in 1 tablespoon thyme, salt and pepper. Remove from the heat. Brush one side of each dough circle with truffle oil. Grill oiled side down on a preheated grill over medium heat for 2 to 3 minutes. Brush the tops with truffle oil and turn over. Sprinkle each pizza with half the cheese, onions and mushrooms. Grill for 8 to 10 minutes or until the crust is golden brown. Remove to a work surface and sprinkle with the remaining 1 tablespoon thyme; drizzle with truffle oil. Cut into wedges and serve.

TEQUILA-LIME CHICKEN AND SWEET CORN PIZZA

1/4 cup tequila
1/2 cup fresh lime juice (from 3 to 4 limes)
1/4 cup fresh orange juice (from 1 orange)
1/2 teaspoon chili powder
1 1/2 teaspoons minced garlic
  (about 1 1/2 cloves)
1/2 teaspoon kosher salt
1/2 teaspoon pepper
1 pound chicken tenders
3 ears fresh yellow corn, husked and cleaned
3 tablespoons olive oil
1 jalapeño chile, seeded and finely chopped
1/4 teaspoon crushed red pepper flakes
1/4 cup thinly sliced chives
1 teaspoon grated lime zest
Additional salt and pepper to taste
Best Pizza Dough (page 76)
Additional olive oil
2 cups (8 ounces) shredded Manchego cheese
Cilantro for garnish

Makes 2 pizzas

Whisk the tequila, lime juice, orange juice, chili powder, garlic, 1/2 teaspoon salt and 1/2 teaspoon pepper in a bowl. Add the chicken and stir to coat. Marinate, covered, in the refrigerator for 3 to 8 hours.

Remove the chicken and discard the marinade. Grill the chicken on a preheated grill for 3 to 5 minutes or until cooked through. Remove the chicken to a work surface and chop. Set aside.

Brush the corn with 1 tablespoon of the olive oil and wrap in foil. Grill the corn for 15 minutes or until tender, turning frequently. Cool. Remove to a work surface and unwrap. Cut the kernels from the cob. Combine the remaining 2 tablespoons olive oil, the corn, jalapeño chile, red pepper flakes, chives and lime zest in a bowl. Season with salt and pepper and mix well.

Brush one side of each dough circle with olive oil. Grill oiled side down on a preheated grill over medium heat for 2 to 3 minutes.

Brush the top side of each pizza with olive oil and turn. Top each with one-quarter of the cheese, half the chicken and half the corn mixture, spreading the ingredients to the edge. Sprinkle evenly with the remaining cheese. Grill for 8 to 10 minutes or until the crust is golden brown. Remove to a work surface and garnish with cilantro. Cut into wedges and serve.

Fig-Prosciutto Pizza with Arugula

Best Pizza Dough (page 76)
Extra-virgin olive oil
1 cup fig jam
1 cup (4 ounces) crumbled Gorgonzola cheese
1 cup (4 ounces) shredded mozzarella cheese
8 slices prosciutto
2 tablespoons balsamic vinegar
1/4 cup (1 ounce) freshly grated
    Parmesan cheese
4 cups arugula

Makes 2 pizzas

*B*rush one side of each dough circle with olive oil. Grill oiled side down on a preheated grill over medium heat for 2 to 3 minutes. Brush the top side of each pizza with olive oil and turn over the pizzas. Spread half the jam to the edge of each pizza and sprinkle with half the Gorgonzola cheese and half the mozzarella cheese. Lay half the prosciutto over each pizza and drizzle with half the vinegar. Grill the pizzas for 8 to 10 minutes or until the crust is golden brown.

Remove to a work surface and sprinkle each pizza with half the Parmesan cheese and half the arugula. Cut into wedges and serve.

Skinny Agave-Rita

1 orange slice
1 lemon slice
2 ounces silver tequila
3/4 ounce Triple Sec
1/4 ounce agave nectar
Juice of 2 limes
Superfine sugar
Soda water
1 lime slice for garnish

Serves 1

*M*uddle the orange and lemon slices in a cocktail shaker. Fill with ice. Add the tequila, liqueur, agave nectar and the lime juice. Shake vigorously. Pour over ice in a 12-ounce glass rimmed with sugar. Top off with soda water. Garnish with a lime slice.

Sweet Grilled Fruit Skewers with Honey Yogurt Sauce

Fruit Skewers

1 1/2 *cups (1/2-inch) pineapple chunks*
1 1/3 *cups seedless red or green grapes*
2 *large peaches, cut into 1/2-inch thick slices*

Serves 8

Honey Yogurt Sauce

6 *ounces plain yogurt*
2 *tablespoons honey*
1 *tablespoon lemon juice*
1/2 *teaspoon vanilla extract*
Dash of cinnamon

Makes 1 cup

*T*hread the pineapple, grapes and peaches alternately onto metal skewers. Grill the skewers on an oiled preheated grill over medium-high heat for 3 to 5 minutes or until the fruit is slightly softened. Serve each skewer with 2 tablespoons of the honey yogurt sauce.

*W*hisk the yogurt, honey, lemon juice, vanilla and cinnamon in a bowl.

Note: If you have fruit and yogurt sauce leftover, combine them with orange or apple juice, a banana and ice in a blender to make a great and healthy fruit shake.

Bastille Day

Serves 6

Montpellier Mussels on the Half Shell

Endive Salad with Roquefort and Walnuts

King Louis XVI Shaved Lemon Beef

Grilled Ratatouille

Tartlette aux Framboise (Raspberry Tart)

Crème Caramel

Fleur-de-Lis Martinis

Bastille Day Menu Sponsored by
Jamie Estes, Estes Public Relations

Tartlette Aux Framboise (Raspberry Tart)

MONTPELLIER MUSSELS ON THE HALF SHELL

HERB BUTTER

1/2 cup (1 stick) butter, softened
1 tablespoon finely chopped fresh parsley
1 tablespoon finely chopped fresh chives
5 teaspoons finely chopped fresh tarragon

Makes 1/2 cup

MUSSELS

24 mussels, scrubbed
1/2 cup dry white wine
1 cup fine bread crumbs

Serves 6

*C*ombine the butter, parsley, chives and tarragon in small bowl and mix well. Set aside.

*R*emove the beard from the mussels by pulling the beard quickly toward the shell hinge with pliers or your fingers. Discard the beards. Tap the shell of any open mussels. Discard any mussels that don't close when tapped.

Place the mussels in a heavy saucepan and add the wine. Cover the pan and bring to a boil over high heat. Reduce the heat and simmer, covered, for 10 minutes. Discard any mussels that remain closed. Remove and discard the top shell from the mussels. Arrange the mussels in a shallow baking pan. Top each one with an equal portion of the herb butter and top with the bread crumbs. Broil for 2 to 4 minutes or until the butter is melted and the bread crumbs are golden brown. Serve warm.

Note: Contrary to what many people think, mussels are relatively inexpensive and easy to make. Keep this little secret to yourself, and your guests will be impressed!

ENDIVE SALAD WITH ROQUEFORT AND WALNUTS

SALAD

4 heads endive
1/4 cup walnuts, coarsely chopped
   and toasted
1/4 cup dried cranberries
1/4 cup crumbled Roquefort or other
   blue cheese

Serves 6

BLUE CHEESE DRESSING

1/3 cup crumbled blue cheese
2 tablespoons plain Greek yogurt
3 tablespoons milk
1 tablespoon chopped chives
1 1/2 teaspoons fresh lemon juice
Salt and pepper to taste

*R*emove several of the outer leaves of the endive. Slice the inner part lengthwise into quarters. Combine the endive and blue cheese dressing in a bowl and toss to coat. Top with the walnuts, cranberries and cheese. Serve on individual salad plates or on a platter.

*P*urée the cheese, yogurt and milk in a blender. Remove to a bowl and stir in the chives, lemon juice, salt and pepper. Chill until ready to use.

*T*he city of Louisville is named after King Louis XVI of France. A statue of the monarch—a gift from Louisville's sister city Montpellier, France—stands tall by Metro Hall in downtown. The fleur-de-lis, a French symbol that can be seen throughout Louisville, including on the city's seal, represents French aid that was given during the Revolutionary War. Need a reason to celebrate? Why not throw a Bastille Day dinner party on or around July 14th and bring a little bit of France to the Bluegrass?

KING LOUIS XVI SHAVED LEMON BEEF

BEEF TENDERLOIN

1 (3-pound) beef tenderloin
Kosher salt and freshly ground pepper
  to taste

Serves 6

Season the beef with salt and pepper and let stand until room temperature. Grill the tenderloin on an oiled preheated grill over medium-high heat for 5 to 6 minutes per side for medium-rare. Remove the beef to a cutting board and let stand for 5 minutes. Slice the beef across the grain into very thin slices.

Arrange on a serving platter and drizzle with the desired amount of lemon basil oil. Serve with crusty French bread and the remaining lemon basil oil for dipping.

LEMON BASIL OIL

Zest and juice of 1 lemon
1/2 teaspoon cracked pepper
1/2 cup extra-virgin olive oil
1/4 cup fresh basil, shredded

Makes 3/4 cup

Combine the lemon zest, lemon juice and pepper in a bowl. Whisk in the olive oil. Stir in the basil. Let stand for at least 1 hour to allow the flavors to mingle.

Think Ashbourne Farms when creating your shopping list for this menu. Their wholesome beef would be perfect for King Louis XVI Lemon Shaved Beef, and their eggs would help make a memorable Crème Caramel (page 87). Their animals are pasture grazed and free of antibiotics and added hormones to ensure the highest quality protein you can provide to your friends and family. Ashbourne's products can be found on their website, at the St. Matthews farmers' market, or at select Paul's Fruit Markets in Louisville.

GRILLED RATATOUILLE

1/4 cup extra-virgin olive oil
2 tablespoons red wine vinegar
2 eggplant, cut into 1/2-inch rounds
3 zucchini, cut lengthwise into 1/2-inch slices
6 plum tomatoes, cut into halves
3 red or yellow bell peppers, seeded and sliced
8 ounces whole mushrooms, trimmed, with
    stems intact
4 thick slices red onion
1 tablespoon extra-virgin olive oil
3 tablespoons minced fresh basil
1 tablespoon minced fresh thyme
1 tablespoon minced garlic
1/2 teaspoon grated lemon zest
1/2 to 3/4 teaspoon kosher salt
1/4 teaspoon freshly ground pepper
Shredded Parmesan cheese or crumbled
    goat cheese for garnish

Serves 6 to 8

*W*hisk 1/4 cup olive oil and the vinegar in a large bowl. Brush some of the vinegar mixture on the eggplant, zucchini, tomatoes, bell peppers, mushrooms and onion. Grill the vegetables on a preheated grill over medium-high heat until tender, noting that grilling times will vary for different vegetables. Chop the tomatoes and zucchini into large pieces and separate the onion slices into rings.

Whisk 1 tablespoon olive oil, the basil, thyme, garlic, lemon zest, salt and pepper into the remaining vinegar mixture. Add the warm zucchini, tomatoes, bell peppers, mushrooms and onion to the vinegar mixture and stir to coat. Arrange the eggplant on a platter and top with the ratatouille. Garnish with cheese and serve.

FLEUR-DE-LIS MARTINIS

1/4 cup sugar
1/2 cup water
1 teaspoon culinary lavender buds
4 cups chopped fresh seedless watermelon
4 ounces gin
4 sprigs of lavender for garnish

Serves 4

*S*immer the sugar, water, and lavender buds in a saucepan over medium heat for about 1 minute or until the sugar dissolves. Remove from the heat and cool to room temperature. Strain the syrup, discarding the buds. Process the watermelon in a blender until smooth. Strain the juice into a large pitcher, discarding the pulp. Add the syrup and gin. Stir in ice. Strain into four martini glasses. Garnish each with a lavender sprig.

Tartlette aux Framboise (Raspberry Tart)

Almond Crust

2/3 cup confectioners' sugar
1/4 cup almonds, ground
1 3/4 cups plus 2 tablespoons all-purpose
   flour, sifted
1/2 cup (1 stick) unsalted butter, softened
1 egg
1 tablespoon (or more) ice water
Additional butter
Additional all-purpose flour

*M*ix the confectioners' sugar and almonds in a bowl. Stir in the flour. Add the butter, egg and 1 tablespoon ice water and mix until the dough sticks together. Add additional ice water 1 teaspoon at a time if the dough is too dry. Shape into a ball. Freeze, wrapped in plastic wrap, for 15 minutes. Butter six 4-inch tart pans and dust with flour. Divide the dough into six balls. Roll out each ball on a floured surface to a 5-inch circle. Fit each circle into a prepared tart pan and trim the edges. Prick the pastry shells all over with a fork. Line each with a 6-inch square of parchment paper and then fill with pie weights or dried beans. Bake in a preheated 350-degree oven for 20 minutes or until golden brown. Remove to a wire rack to cool completely. Remove the parchment and pie weights.

Filling

8 ounces mascarpone cheese, softened
1/2 cup plain Greek yogurt
4 1/2 tablespoons confectioners' sugar
Seeds from 1 vanilla bean
16 ounces fresh raspberries
3/4 cup salted pistachios, shelled and
   coarsely chopped

Serves 6

*W*hisk the cheese, yogurt, confectioners' sugar and vanilla seeds in a bowl until thick and smooth. Spoon about 2 tablespoons of the cheese mixture evenly into each cooled tart shell. Arrange equal portions of the raspberries in an attractive low mound on top of each tart and sprinkle with the pistachios. Chill at least 15 minutes. Remove from the tart pans to serve.

Variations: To keep from buying additional ingredients and to switch things up, try substituting chopped almonds for the pistachios. If using unsalted almonds, add a pinch of salt before sprinkling over the raspberries.

CRÈME CARAMEL

CARAMEL SAUCE
1 pound sugar (about 2 cups)
1/2 cup water
1/4 cup rum

Makes about 1 cup

CUSTARD
6 egg yolks
1/2 cup packed brown sugar
1 pint (2 cups) heavy cream
1/2 teaspoon coffee extract
Mint leaves for garnish

Serves 8

Note: If you've never tempered eggs before, don't stress. It's very easy. The goal is to add hot liquid to the egg mixture very slowly to avoid creating scrambled eggs. Start by adding a small amount of the hot liquid to the eggs while stirring briskly. Once well incorporated, add the remaining hot liquid slowly, again while stirring.

Chef: Chef Alexander Dulaney, Bistro Le Relais

*C*ook the sugar in a nonreactive saucepan over medium heat for 10 to 15 minutes or until the sugar is melted and turns a copper color, stirring occasionally with a wooden spoon. Remove from the heat and stir in the water and rum carefully and slowly as the sugar may spatter. Return the mixture to a boil and cook until smooth, stirring constantly. Remove from the heat and cool completely.

*W*hisk the egg yolks and brown sugar in a bowl. Heat the cream in a saucepan to almost boiling. Temper the eggs by whisking a small amount of the cream into the eggs. Whisk in the remaining cream very slowly, whisking constantly. Stir in the coffee extract. Pour 2 tablespoons of the caramel sauce into each of eight (8-ounce) ramekins and swirl to lightly coat the bottom and side. Pour equal portions of the custard into each ramekin. Place the ramekins in a baking pan. Add enough hot water to the baking pan to come halfway up the side of the ramekins.

Bake in the lower third of a preheated 325-degree oven for 1 1/2 hours or until a knife inserted in the center of the custard comes out clean. Remove the ramekins to a wire rack to cool completely. Cover the ramekins with plastic wrap and chill for at least 3 hours. Run a small sharp knife around the edge of the ramekins to loosen. Invert the each ramekin onto a serving plate. Garnish with mint and serve.

Farmers' Market

Serves 6

SWEET-AND-SALTY HONEY CHEESE SPREAD

NULU GARDEN GREENS VICHYSSOISE

BARDSTOWN ROAD GRILLED CHICKEN WITH
RED PEPPERS AND CARAMELIZED CORN

CRESCENT HILL EGGPLANT PARMESAN ROLLS WITH SWISS CHARD

DOUGLASS LOOP BASIL CARROTS

BLUE RIBBON PEACHES AND CREAM CAKE

GREEN TOMATO BROWN BETTY WITH SWEET CORN ICE CREAM

LEMON BASILICA

Farmers' Market Menu Sponsored by

Solberg Manufacturing Inc.

Douglass Loop Basil Carrots

SWEET-AND-SALTY HONEY CHEESE SPREAD

1/2 cup salted sunflower kernels,
  lightly toasted
1 1/2 tablespoons finely chopped fresh mint
1 (10-ounce) log goat cheese
1/3 cup honey
1 pint fresh raspberries
Additional mint leaves for garnish

Serves 6 to 8

Mix the sunflower kernels and 1 1/2 tablespoons mint together. Coat the cheese in the mixture, including the ends. Place the cheese on a serving platter and chill until ready to serve.

Drizzle the cheese with the honey. Sprinkle with the raspberries and garnish with additional mint. Serve with crackers.

NuLu GARDEN GREENS VICHYSSOISE

2 tablespoons butter
3 potatoes, peeled and chopped
3 leeks, trimmed and chopped
2 cups fresh spinach or peeled
  chopped zucchini
4 cups vegetable stock
1 teaspoon salt
1 teaspoon pepper
1/2 cup (or more) cream
1/4 cup chopped chives for garnish
1 tablespoon olive oil for garnish

Serves 6

Melt the butter in a stockpot. Add the potatoes, leeks and spinach and sauté for 3 minutes or until the vegetables soften. Stir in the stock, salt and pepper. Bring to a boil over medium-high heat. Reduce the heat and cover. Simmer for 20 minutes or until the vegetables are tender. Remove from the heat. Purée the mixture with an immersion blender or in batches in a countertop blender. Remove to a bowl and chill until cold. Stir in the cream, adding more cream if the soup is too thick. Ladle into serving bowls and garnish with the chives and a drizzle of olive oil.

BARDSTOWN ROAD GRILLED CHICKEN WITH RED PEPPERS AND CARAMELIZED CORN

CHICKEN

6 tablespoons fresh lemon juice
2 tablespoons balsamic vinegar
1/4 cup olive oil
1/2 cup chicken stock
2 garlic cloves, minced
6 boneless skinless chicken breasts
2 red bell peppers, cut into halves
2 yellow bell peppers, cut into halves
2 green bell peppers, cut into halves
2 zucchini, cut into halves lengthwise
Salt and pepper to taste
1 cup balsamic vinegar
16 basil leaves, minced for garnish

Serves 6

*W*hisk the lemon juice, 2 tablespoons vinegar, the olive oil, stock and garlic in a shallow bowl. Add the chicken and turn to coat. Marinate in the refrigerator for at least 1 hour.

Grill the bell peppers and zucchini on a preheated grill until tender. Remove to a work surface to cool. Cut into strips and season with salt and pepper.

Remove the chicken from the marinade, discarding the marinade. Grill the chicken on a preheated 400-degree grill for 7 minutes per side or until cooked through.

Cook 1 cup vinegar in a saucepan over medium heat until reduced by half and the consistency of syrup. Divide the caramelized corn among six serving plates and top each with one chicken breast. Top with equal portions of the grilled bell peppers and zucchini. Drizzle with the vinegar syrup and garnish with basil.

CARAMELIZED CORN

1/4 cup (1/2 stick) unsalted butter
3 cups corn kernels (from about 6 ears corn)
6 large shallots, thinly sliced
1 teaspoon sugar
1/4 teaspoon cayenne pepper
Pinch of red pepper flakes
Salt and black pepper to taste
1 tablespoon chopped fresh thyme
1 garlic clove or large garlic scape, minced

Serves 6

*M*elt the butter in a large skillet over medium heat. Stir in the corn, shallots, sugar, cayenne pepper, red pepper flakes, salt and black pepper. Cook for 20 to 25 minutes or until the corn caramelizes, stirring frequently. Add the thyme and garlic and cook for 5 minutes, stirring frequently.

CRESCENT HILL EGGPLANT PARMESAN ROLLS WITH SWISS CHARD

TOMATO SAUCE

1 tablespoon olive oil
1 small onion, finely chopped
3 garlic cloves, chopped
1 carrot, peeled and chopped
1/2 teaspoon sea salt
1/2 teaspoon pepper
1 (16-ounce) can crushed tomatoes
2 bay leaves
Additional sea salt and pepper to taste

Makes 2 cups

EGGPLANT

2 (1 1/2-pound) eggplant, sliced lengthwise
   1/4- to 1/2-inch thick
2 tablespoons kosher salt
3 tablespoons olive oil

*L*ayer the eggplant slices over the bottom and up the side of two colanders, sprinkling each layer with some of the salt, using all of the eggplant and salt. Set each colander over a bowl and let stand for 30 minutes to 1 hour.

SWISS CHARD FILLING

16 ounces Swiss chard, stalks removed
2 eggs
Pinch of salt
15 ounces whole milk ricotta cheese
1/4 cup (1 ounce) grated Parmesan cheese
2 tablespoons chopped mint
1 tablespoon pepper

*H*eat the olive oil in a saucepan over medium-high heat. Add the onion and garlic and sauté for 10 minutes or until the onion is translucent. Add the carrot, 1/2 teaspoon salt and 1/2 teaspoon pepper and sauté for 10 minutes. Stir in the tomatoes and bay leaves and reduce the heat to low. Simmer for 1 hour or until the sauce thickens. Remove and discard the bay leaves. Season with salt and pepper to taste. Remove to a bowl and let cool. Chill, covered, for up to 24 hours, if desired.

Rinse the eggplant slices and pat dry with paper towels. Arrange the eggplant in a single layer in three parchment-lined shallow baking pans. Brush both sides of the slices with the olive oil. Broil one baking pan 5 to 6 inches from the heat source under a preheated broiler for 3 to 4 minutes or until tender and beginning to brown. Remove and cool the eggplant to room temperature. Repeat with the remaining eggplant.

*A*dd the Swiss chard to a large saucepan of boiling salted water and boil for 2 minutes or just until tender. Drain in a colander and rinse with cold water to stop the cooking process. Squeeze the chard dry and chop coarsely. Squeeze the chopped chard between paper towels to dry thoroughly. Whisk the eggs and salt in a bowl. Stir in the chard, ricotta cheese, Parmesan cheese, mint and pepper.

ASSEMBLY

8 ounces mozzarella cheese, cut into
thin slices
¹/4 cup (1 ounce) grated Parmesan cheese

Serves 6

Reheat the tomato sauce if chilled. Spread half the tomato sauce over the bottom of an oiled 10×15-inch baking dish. Spoon equal portions of the Swiss chard filling in the center of each eggplant slice. Roll up the eggplant loosely, enclosing the filling. Arrange the rolls seam side down in the baking dish. Spoon the remaining tomato sauce over the rolls and lay the mozzarella cheese over the top in a single layer. Sprinkle with the Parmesan cheese. Bake, covered with foil, in a preheated 350-degree oven for 30 minutes or until heated through. Bake, uncovered, for 15 to 20 minutes longer or until the sauce is bubbly.

Note: This can be made up to 24 hours in advance and refrigerated. Bring to room temperature before baking and increase the baking time by 10 minutes.

DOUGLASS LOOP BASIL CARROTS

1 pound carrots, peeled and sliced, or 1 pound
baby carrots
2 tablespoons butter, melted
1 tablespoon lemon juice
¹/2 teaspoon garlic salt
1 teaspoon chopped fresh basil
Dash of pepper

Serves 6

Cook the carrots in a saucepan of boiling water for 8 to 10 minutes or until tender-crisp; drain. Remove to a serving bowl. Whisk the melted butter, lemon juice and garlic salt in a bowl. Drizzle over the carrots. Sprinkle with the basil and pepper.

Note: This is a perfect side dish for pork tenderloin or chicken.

BLUE RIBBON PEACHES AND CREAM CAKE

CAKE

2 1/4 cups cake flour, sifted
1 cup plus 6 tablespoons sugar, sifted
2 teaspoons baking powder
1/2 teaspoon salt
1/2 cup vegetable oil
7 egg yolks
1/3 cup bottled peach syrup
1/3 cup water
1/2 teaspoon vanilla extract
1/2 teaspoon almond extract
10 egg whites
1 1/4 teaspoons cream of tartar
2 tablespoons sugar

Serves 12

Combine the flour, 1 cup plus 6 tablespoons sugar, the baking powder and salt in a mixing bowl and beat for 1 minute. Make a well in the center of the flour mixture. Add the oil, egg yolks, peach syrup, water, vanilla and almond extract to the well and beat until smooth.

PEACH FROSTING

12 ounces cream cheese, softened
6 tablespoons butter, softened
1 1/4 cups confectioners' sugar, sifted
1 teaspoon vanilla extract
1/4 teaspoon almond extract
1 tablespoon bottled peach syrup
3/4 cup heavy whipping cream, chilled
1 tablespoon bottled peach syrup
3/4 cup confectioners' sugar, sifted

Beat the egg whites in a mixing bowl until frothy. Add the cream of tartar and beat until soft peaks form. Add 2 tablespoons sugar and beat until stiff peaks form. Fold the egg whites into the batter. Pour the batter evenly into four greased and floured 9-inch cake pans. Run a small knife through the batter to remove any air bubbles. Bake in a preheated 350-degree oven for 25 minutes or until wooden picks inserted in the centers come out clean and the cakes spring back when lightly touched in the center. Cool in the pans for 10 minutes. Remove to a wire rack to cool completely. Place one cooled cake layer on a serving plate and spread with a thin layer of the frosting. Spread one-third of the peach filling over the frosting and top with one-third of the peach cream. Repeat the layers two more times and top with the final cake layer. Spread the remaining frosting over the top and side of the cake.

Beat the cream cheese, butter, 1 1/4 cups confectioners' sugar, the vanilla, almond extract and 1 tablespoon peach syrup in a mixing bowl until smooth. Beat the cream, 1 tablespoon peach syrup and 3/4 cup confectioners' sugar in another mixing bowl until medium peaks form. Fold into the cream cheese mixture one-third at a time. Chill until firm but spreadable.

PEACH FILLING

1/2 cup sugar
1/2 vanilla bean, cut into 1-inch pieces
4 cups sliced peeled peaches
2 tablespoons water
2 tablespoons all-purpose flour
1/4 cup sugar
1/2 teaspoon almond extract

PEACH CREAM

3 cups sliced peeled peaches
1 1/2 teaspoons lemon juice
1/2 teaspoon almond extract
1/4 teaspoon vanilla extract
2 1/2 teaspoons unflavored gelatin
7 tablespoons sugar
2 cups heavy whipping cream

Process 1/2 cup sugar and the vanilla bean in a food processor until the vanilla bean is ground. Sift the sugar through a wire mesh strainer into a large bowl and discard any large vanilla bean pieces. Add the peaches, water, flour and 1/4 cup sugar and toss to coat. Remove to a saucepan. Cook until bubbly, breaking up the peaches with the back of a spoon. Remove from the heat and cool completely. Stir in the almond extract.

Purée the peaches in a food processor. Press the peaches through a wire mesh strainer into a heavy saucepan and discard any solids in the strainer. Stir the lemon juice into the peach purée. Simmer until the peach mixture is reduced to 1 cup. Remove from the heat and let cool. Stir in the almond and vanilla extracts. Spoon 1/4 cup of the peach purée into a heatproof measuring cup and sprinkle with the gelatin. Let stand for 5 minutes. Set the measuring cup into a pan of simmering water. Heat for a few minutes or until the gelatin is dissolved, stirring occasionally. Combine the remaining peach purée, gelatin mixture and sugar in a bowl and mix well. Beat the cream in a chilled mixing bowl until soft peaks form. Add the peach mixture and beat until stiff peaks form.

Note: This cake won First Place for Favorite Cake in the Kentucky State Fair by Junior League Sustainer, Maria Fisher.

Green Tomato Brown Betty with Sweet Corn Ice Cream

Green Tomato Brown Betty

1 tablespoon butter
8 green tomatoes, chopped
1/2 cup packed brown sugar
1/4 cup granulated sugar
2 teaspoons vanilla extract
1 tablespoon apple pie spice
1 tablespoon cinnamon
1/2 cup orange juice
2 tablespoons arrowroot or cornstarch
1 cup packed brown sugar
1/2 cup all-purpose flour
1/2 cup rolled oats
2 teaspoons salt
1 tablespoon cinnamon
1/2 cup (1 stick) cold butter, cut into pieces

Serves 6 to 8

Melt 1 tablespoon butter in a large skillet over medium-high heat. Add the tomatoes, 1/2 cup brown sugar, the granulated sugar, vanilla, apple pie spice and 1 tablespoon cinnamon. Cook for 3 to 5 minutes or until the tomatoes begin to release their juice, stirring frequently. Whisk the orange juice and arrowroot together in a bowl. Whisk slowly into the tomatoes. Cook for 5 to 8 minutes or until thickened, stirring frequently. Pour the mixture into a greased 8×12-inch baking dish. Combine 1 cup brown sugar, the flour, oats, salt and 1 tablespoon cinnamon in a bowl and mix well. Add 1/2 cup cold butter and mix with clean hands until crumbly. Sprinkle over the tomato mixture. Bake in a preheated 350-degree oven for 20 to 25 minutes or until golden brown. Serve with sweet corn ice cream.

Note: To save time, you may serve this with vanilla ice cream instead.

Support the local food and farming communities by shopping neighborhood famers' markets. Kentucky has over 150 markets and 2,000 vendors, and the numbers keep rising. Farmers' markets in the Commonwealth generate an estimated $11 million in annual sales for local farmers. These markets can be found in all areas of the city—the Highlands, St. Matthews, Lyndon, southwest Louisville, and Old Louisville—and take place on a variety of days each week. Learn more about buying select produce in Kentucky by turning to page 198.

Sweet Corn Ice Cream

1/2 cup milk
1/2 cup whipping cream
1 (2-inch) vanilla bean, split
3 egg yolks
3 tablespoons sugar
5 ears of fresh corn, grilled and kernels
    cut from the cob

Makes 1 pint

Combine the milk and cream in a saucepan. Scrape the seeds from the vanilla bean into the milk mixture and add the bean. Bring to a simmer and then remove from the heat. Remove the vanilla bean. Whisk the egg yolks and sugar in a bowl. Whisk the hot milk mixture into the egg yolks gradually. Pour the milk and egg mixture into the saucepan. Cook over low heat for 5 minutes or until thickened and the mixture coats the back of a spoon, stirring constantly. Do not let boil. Strain through a mesh strainer into a bowl and discard the solids. Chill, covered, until cold. Process the custard with the corn in a blender until smooth. Pour into an ice cream freezer container. Freeze using the manufacturer's directions. Freeze until ready to serve.

Chef: Chef Tyson Long, Winston's Restaurant

Lemon Basilica

2 basil leaves
2 cucumber slices
Juice of 1 lemon
2 ounces gin
3/4 cup elderflower liquor
2 ounces Prosecco
Lemon wedge and basil leaf for garnish

Serves 1

Muddle 2 basil leaves, the cucumber and lemon juice in a cocktail shaker. Fill with ice. Add the gin and liqueur. Shake vigorously for 10 seconds and then strain into a martini glass. Top off with the Prosecco. Garnish with a lemon wedge and basil leaf.

Cool Down Salad Party

Serves 6

SWEET SUMMER TOMATO BITES

TARRAGON CHICKEN SALAD CUPS

FRESH WATERMELON CUCUMBER SALAD

TABOULI SALAD WITH LAMB MEATBALLS AND CUCUMBER YOGURT SAUCE

ZESTY DILL AND ZUCCHINI SOUTHERN CORN MUFFINS

GRATEFUL GREEN BEAN AND PEA PANZANELLA

BERRY MACAROON DELIGHT

GRAPEFRUIT GRANITA

Cool Down Salad Party Menu Sponsored by

PriceWeber

 PriceWeber

Fresh Watermelon Cucumber Salad

SWEET SUMMER TOMATO BITES

2/3 cup mayonnaise
1/2 cup fresh basil
1/4 cup fresh chives
1/2 teaspoon kosher salt
1/4 teaspoon freshly ground pepper
6 small tomatoes, such as Roma tomatoes
6 to 12 slices whole grain bread
Chopped fresh basil for garnish

Serves 12

Combine the mayonnaise, 1/2 cup basil, the chives, salt and pepper in a small food processor or blender. Pulse until well mixed and the herbs are chopped. Slice the tomatoes to yield at least 24 tomato slices. Cut the bread with a cookie cutter or small biscuit cutter to yield tomato-size bread rounds. Spread equal portions of the herbed mayonnaise on the bread and top each with a tomato slice. Garnish with chopped basil and serve.

Variation: Try different herbs for a varied taste. You may substitute cucumber slices for the tomatoes. For bite-size appetizers, cut the bread into smaller rounds and use cherry tomatoes.

TARRAGON CHICKEN SALAD CUPS

24 slices whole wheat or white bread
3/4 cup mayonnaise
1 tablespoon chopped fresh tarragon
1 teaspoon grated lemon zest
1 tablespoon fresh lemon juice
1 teaspoon salt
1/2 teaspoon pepper
1/2 cup pecans, toasted and chopped
3 cups chopped cooked chicken
2 ribs celery, finely chopped
1/2 small sweet onion, finely chopped
2 cups seedless red grapes, cut into halves

Serves 4 to 6

Trim the crusts from the bread to make 4×4-inch bread squares. Roll each bread slice on a work surface with a rolling pin to flatten. Press the bread squares into nonstick miniature muffin cups so that the four corners of the bread are exposed at the top of the muffin cup. Bake in a preheated 350-degree oven for 5 to 10 minutes or until the edges are light brown. Remove the bread cups to a wire rack to cool completely. Combine the mayonnaise, tarragon, lemon zest, lemon juice, salt and pepper in a bowl and mix well. Add the pecans, chicken, celery and onion and gently mix. Fold in the grapes. Fill the bread cups with the chicken salad and serve.

FRESH WATERMELON CUCUMBER SALAD

WATERMELON SALAD

4 cups chopped seedless watermelon
1/2 large red onion, thinly sliced
1 large seedless cucumber, chopped
2 tablespoons finely chopped fresh mint
3/4 cup kalamata olives, pitted
4 ounces feta cheese, crumbled
1/2 teaspoon sea salt
Mint sprigs for garnish

Serves 6

BALSAMIC VINAIGRETTE

1/4 cup extra-virgin olive oil
2 1/2 tablespoons balsamic vinegar
1 teaspoon brown sugar
1/4 teaspoon salt
1/4 teaspoon pepper

Makes 1/3 cup

*P*at the watermelon, onion and cucumber dry with paper towels and place in a bowl. Add the chopped mint and toss to mix. Add the olives, cheese and salt and toss to mix. Add the balsamic vinaigrette and toss gently to coat. Garnish with fresh mint sprigs.

*W*hisk the olive oil, vinegar, brown sugar, salt and pepper in a bowl.

Note: This salad is attractive served in clear martini glasses.

*H*osting a salad party is one of the simplest ways to entertain. You provide the lettuce and a dressing "bar," and ask your friends to bring two to three of their favorite toppings. To get people to think outside the box, have guests vote on the most unique topping and provide the winner with a bottle of gourmet dressing, a wooden salad bowl, or a pair of locally crafted tongs. It will be the perfect party to cool down on a hot Kentucky night.

TABOULI SALAD WITH LAMB MEATBALLS AND CUCUMBER YOGURT SAUCE

LAMB MEATBALLS

1 pound ground lamb
1 tablespoon minced parsley
2 teaspoons minced thyme
3 garlic cloves, grated
1 egg
1/4 cup matzo meal
1 teaspoon salt, or to taste
1 teaspoon pepper, or to taste
3 tablespoons matzo meal
2 tablespoons olive oil
Crumbled feta cheese for garnish

Serves 6 to 8

*C*ombine the lamb, parsley, thyme, garlic, egg, 1/4 cup matzo meal, salt and pepper in a bowl and mix well. Shape into 1-inch balls. Coat the meatballs in 3 tablespoons matzo meal. Heat the olive oil in a heavy skillet over medium heat. Add the meatballs in small batches and cook until golden brown and cooked through. Remove the meatballs to paper towels to drain. Mound the tabouli on a large platter and top with the meatballs. Drizzle with the cucumber yogurt sauce and garnish with feta cheese.

TABOULI

1 cup bulgur wheat
1/4 cup lemon juice, or to taste
1/4 cup (or more) extra-virgin olive oil
3 garlic cloves, minced
2 teaspoons ground sumac or paprika
2 cups chopped curly parsley
1/4 cup chopped mint
1 white onion, finely chopped
1 seedless cucumber, peeled and chopped
   into 1/4-inch cubes
3 plum tomatoes, seeded and chopped into
   1/4-inch cubes
Salt and freshly ground pepper to taste

Serves 6 to 8

*P*lace the bulgur in a fine mesh strainer and rinse well. Remove to a bowl and cover with cool water. Let stand for 30 to 60 minutes to soften. Drain well and set aside. Whisk the lemon juice, olive oil, garlic and sumac in a large bowl. Stir in the parsley and mint. Fold in the bulgur gently in batches. Fold in the onion, cucumber and tomato. Season with salt and pepper and add more lemon juice and olive oil if needed. Serve within 4 hours at room temperature or chill for up to 3 days.

Note: Ground sumac can be found at specialty spice stores.

CUCUMBER YOGURT SAUCE

1 cucumber
2 cups plain Greek yogurt
1/4 cup dill weed, finely chopped
1/4 cup mint, finely chopped
1 tablespoon tahini
1 tablespoon honey, or to taste
1 tablespoon lemon juice, or to taste
Salt and pepper to taste

Makes 2 1/2 cups

*P*eel the cucumber and remove the seeds. Grate the cucumber and place in a fine mesh sieve to drain well. Combine the cucumber, yogurt, dill weed and mint in a bowl and mix well. Add the tahini, honey, lemon juice, salt and pepper and mix well. Chill up to 3 days.

Chef: Casey Broussard, Wiltshire Pantry

*T*he Junior League of Louisville proudly supports the Be Fit, Be Fine Health and Wellness Initiative *through urban gardening—the act of cultivating, processing, and distributing food grown in or around an urban area—and cooking classes at Family Scholar House (FSH). FSH's mission is to end the cycle of poverty by giving single-parent students the support they need to earn a four-year college degree. Our cooking classes help parents cook healthy meals on a budget. We encourage the utilization of the vegetables and herbs from our gardens. Our chef and the committee create easy recipes in hopes of bringing family meals back to people's daily lives. Be Fit, Be Fine addresses today's health challenges at the root of the cause: staying active, making healthy food choices, and teaching the best gardening practices.*

ZESTY DILL AND ZUCCHINI SOUTHERN CORN MUFFINS

1³/4 cups stone-ground cornmeal
1 tablespoon sugar
1 teaspoon baking powder
1 teaspoon baking soda
1 teaspoon salt
4 teaspoons chopped fresh dill weed
2 eggs
2 cups buttermilk
2 cups peeled grated zucchini
1 cup corn kernels

Makes 12

*W*hisk the cornmeal, sugar, baking powder, baking soda, salt and dill weed in a bowl. Whisk the eggs in a bowl until frothy. Whisk in the buttermilk. Add to the dry ingredients and stir until combined. Fold in the zucchini and corn. Spoon into greased or paper-lined muffin cups. Bake in a preheated 450-degree oven for 20 to 25 minutes. Remove to a wire rack to cool.

Note: Store any leftovers muffins in a sealed container to prevent drying. Warm the muffins before serving.

GRATEFUL GREEN BEAN AND PEA PANZANELLA

4 slices dry rustic bread, cut into 1-inch cubes
1 tablespoon chopped garlic
¹/4 cup olive oil
Salt and pepper to taste
1 cup fava beans, shelled
1 cup French-style green beans, cut into
   bite-size pieces
1 cup each fresh green peas and sugar snap peas
¹/2 cup olive oil
¹/4 cup red wine vinegar
1¹/2 teaspoons Dijon mustard
6 cups salad greens, such as arugula
   or spinach
¹/2 cup thinly sliced red onion
¹/2 cup fresh basil, chopped

Serves 6 to 8

*B*ake the bread on a baking sheet in a preheated 375-degree oven for 14 minutes or until golden brown, turning once. Cool on a wire rack for several minutes. Sauté the garlic in ¹/4 cup olive oil in a saucepan over medium-low heat for 3 minutes. Pour over the bread and toss to coat. Season with salt and pepper. Blanch the beans and peas in a saucepan of boiling salted water for 1 minute or until tender-crisp. Drain and plunge into an ice water bath to stop the cooking process. Drain and dry well. Whisk ¹/2 cup olive oil, the vinegar and Dijon mustard in a bowl and season with salt and pepper. Combine the greens, beans, peas, onion, basil and bread cubes in a large bowl and toss to mix. Add the desired amount of vinaigrette and toss to coat.

BERRY MACAROON DELIGHT

1 quart vanilla ice cream, softened
10 ounces strawberries
6 coconut macaroons, broken
1/4 cup Kentucky bourbon
Fresh strawberries for garnish

Serves 8

Combine the ice cream, 10 ounces strawberries, cookies and bourbon in a bowl and mix well. Spoon into a mold and freeze until firm. Unmold onto a serving plate and garnish with fresh strawberries.

Note: This recipe was originally featured in the Junior League of Louisville's first cookbook, The Cooking Book.

GRAPEFRUIT GRANITA

1 cup granulated sugar
1 cup water
1 cup packed basil leaves, chopped
1 cup grapefruit juice
1 cup vodka

Serves 4

Combine the sugar and water in a small saucepan and simmer until the sugar has completely dissolved, stirring occasionally. Bring to just under a boil. The syrup should be clear, not cloudy; let cool slighty. Stir in the basil. Let steep for 30 minutes and then strain into freezer-safe container. Stir in the grapefruit juice and vodka. Chill in the freezer until just slightly frozen. Spoon into glasses to serve.

Fall

Ashview Farm

Fall

Ashview Farm—a 350-acre horse farm in Versailles, Kentucky—is dedicated to the tradition of breeding, raising, buying, and selling thoroughbred horses. Owners Mr. and Mrs. Wayne G. Lyster III graciously donated their beautiful land (and some of their four-legged friends) for this chic, southern picnic in the heart of the Bluegrass. Re-create this table setting in your own backyard by incorporating an assortment of pine cones and flowers on the center of a plaid tablecloth. Mason jars, as a substitute for dinner glasses, offer a unique and fun twist for a casual fall gathering.

FALL MENUS

Fall Chapter Sponsored by

Yum! Brands Foundation

Tailgating

Serves 8 to 10

KALE AND SAUSAGE BITES

KICK-OFF CARAMELIZED ONION DIP

ROASTED CHICKPEAS

KENTUCKY BISON BURGER WITH
APPLEWOOD-SMOKED BACON AND JEZEBEL SAUCE

RED ZONE CHILI

TOUCHDOWN CRUNCH SLAW

SWEET POTATO SALAD

UK VS. UofL GOVERNOR'S CUP CUPCAKES

SIDELINED CIDER

Red Zone Chili

KALE AND SAUSAGE BITES

KALE AND SAUSAGE BITES

2 tablespoons butter
1 large bunch kale, stemmed and chopped
Splash of vinegar
1/2 onion, finely chopped
1 pound bulk sausage
3/4 cup bread crumbs
1/2 cup (2 ounces) grated Parmesan cheese
2 eggs
2 teaspoons garlic powder
1 teaspoon cumin
2 teaspoons basil
2 teaspoons oregano
Red pepper to taste

Serves 8

BOURBON GLAZE

3/4 cup apple jelly
6 tablespoons spicy brown mustard
2 teaspoons Worcestershire sauce
1/3 cup Kentucky bourbon
1/8 teaspoon crushed red pepper flakes

Makes 1 1/2 cups

*M*elt the butter in a skillet. Add the kale, vinegar and onion and sauté until the kale and onion are tender. Remove to a large bowl. Brown the sausage in the skillet, stirring until crumbly; drain. Add the sausage, bread crumbs, cheese, eggs, garlic powder, cumin, basil, oregano and red pepper to the kale mixture and mix well.

Shape into 1 1/2-inch balls and arrange in a shallow baking pan. Bake in a preheated 400-degree oven for 20 minutes or until crisp. Remove to a serving platter and serve with bourbon glaze on the side for dipping or add the meatballs to the bourbon glaze and simmer over low heat for 8 to 10 minutes or until the sauce thickens slightly, stirring occasionally.

*C*ombine the jelly, mustard, Worcestershire sauce, bourbon and crushed red pepper in a large nonstick skillet. Cook over medium heat until the jelly is melted and the mixture boils, stirring constantly.

SIDELINED CIDER

4 (12-ounce) bottles lager, chilled
1 (25-ounce) bottle sparkling apple
   cider, chilled
1 cup cranberry juice

Serves 4 to 6

*P*our the beer into a pitcher slowly. Add the sparkling cider and cranberry juice gradually. Pour into frosted glasses and serve immediately.

KICK-OFF CARAMELIZED ONION DIP

1/4 cup olive oil
1/4 cup (1/2 stick) butter
2 large Vidalia onions, cut into 1/8-inch slices
2 shallots, chopped
1 teaspoon salt
1/2 teaspoon black pepper
1/4 teaspoon cayenne pepper
2 garlic cloves, chopped
4 ounces cream cheese, softened
1/2 cup mayonnaise
1/2 cup sour cream
3 slices bacon, crisp-cooked and crumbled

Serves 8

*H*eat the olive oil and butter in a large skillet over medium heat. Add the onions, shallots, salt, black pepper and cayenne pepper and sauté for 10 minutes. Reduce the heat to medium-low and cook for 20 minutes or until the onions are golden brown and caramelized, stirring occasionally. Add the garlic and sauté for 45 seconds. Remove to a bowl and cool to room temperature. Beat the cream cheese, mayonnaise and sour cream in bowl until smooth. Add the onion mixture and bacon and mix well. Serve at room temperature.

Note: Pair with potato chips, baguettes, or crudités to win over all of your guests!

ROASTED CHICKPEAS

3 tablespoons olive oil
2 tablespoons ground cumin
1 tablespoon chili powder
2 teaspoons garlic powder
2 teaspoons onion powder
1 teaspoon cayenne pepper, or more to taste
1 1/2 teaspoons sea salt
1 teaspoon black pepper
2 (15-ounce) cans chickpeas, rinsed, drained and patted dry

Serves 10

*W*hisk the olive oil, cumin, chili powder, garlic powder, onion powder, cayenne pepper, salt and black pepper in a bowl. Add the chickpeas and toss to coat. Spread in a single layer in a shallow baking pan lined with foil. Bake in a preheated 400-degree oven for 40 to 50 minutes or until crunchy, stirring every 5 to 10 minutes. Remove to a wire rack to cool. Serve warm or at room temperature. Cool completely before storing in an airtight container.

Variation: Add a handful of wasabi peas to kick up the flavor and add a pop of color.

KENTUCKY BISON BURGER WITH APPLEWOOD-SMOKED BACON AND JEZEBEL SAUCE

BURGER

4 pounds ground bison, shaped into
*   8 (1/2-pound) patties*
Salt and freshly ground pepper to taste
16 slices thick-cut applewood bacon,
*   crisp-cooked*
16 slices aged Cheddar cheese
1 head frisée lettuce
2 tablespoons minced parsley
2 tablespoons minced chives
2 tablespoons minced shallots
2 teaspoons lemon juice
2 tablespoons extra-virgin olive oil
8 kaiser rolls, challah buns or preferred
*   burger buns*

Serves 8

JEZEBEL SAUCE

2 cups each apricot preserves and apple jelly
1 1/2 cups horseradish
1 tablespoon kosher salt
1 1/2 teaspoons pepper
1 1/2 teaspoons ground coriander
2 teaspoons ground cinnamon
1 teaspoon grated nutmeg
1/2 teaspoon grated cloves

Makes 4 cups

Combine the apricot preserves, apple jelly, horseradish, salt, pepper, coriander, cinnamon, nutmeg and cloves in a bowl and mix well. Store, tightly sealed, in the refrigerator.

Season the bison patties generously with salt and paper. Place on a well greased grill rack on a preheated grill. Turn the patties one-quarter after 5 minutes. Grill for 8 minutes per side for medium-rare. Top each with two slices of the bacon and two slices of the cheese and grill until the cheese is melted. Remove to a platter and keep warm. Combine the frisée, parsley, chives, shallots, lemon juice, olive oil, salt and pepper in a bowl and toss to mix. Toast the buns lightly on the grill and remove to a work surface. Place one cooked patty on the bottom of each bun. Top with equal potions of the frisée salad and top each with 1 tablespoon Jezebel sauce. Cover with the bun tops. Serve immediately.

Chef: Chef Levon Wallace, Proof on Main

This burger is comprised of local bison meat from the Kentucky Bison Co. Their buffalo are raised on Woodland Farm in Goshen, Kentucky, without the use of steroids, stimulants, or sub-therapeutic antibiotics. Kentucky Bison Co. buffalo can be found on their website, local specialty food shops, and select farmers' markets.

114

RED ZONE CHILI

2 teaspoons olive oil
2 green or yellow bell peppers, chopped
1 1/2 cups chopped onions
1 tablespoon minced garlic
4 (14-ounce) cans diced tomatoes
2 (15-ounce) cans dark red kidney beans,
    rinsed and drained
2 cups dry red lentils, rinsed and drained
1/4 cup chili powder
2 teaspoons ground cumin
1/2 teaspoon ancho chili powder, or to taste
3 cups water
Hot red pepper sauce to taste
1 (8-ounce) can tomato sauce
1 (6-ounce) can tomato paste
1/8 teaspoon pepper
2 cups (8 ounces) shredded Cheddar
    cheese (optional)
Tortilla chips (optional)
Sour cream (optional)

Serves 6

*H*eat the olive oil in a heavy 8-quart saucepan. Add the bell peppers, onions and garlic and sauté until the vegetables are tender. Stir in the undrained tomatoes, kidney beans, lentils, chili powder, cumin, ancho chili powder, water and hot sauce. Bring to a boil. Reduce the heat and cook, covered, for 30 minutes or until the lentils are tender.

Stir in the tomato sauce, tomato paste and pepper. Cook until hot, stirring occasionally. Ladle into serving bowls and top with the cheese, tortilla chips and sour cream. Store any leftover chili in the refrigerator for up to 3 days. The flavors enhance overnight.

*T*he most intense college rivalry in the Commonwealth and, as some would argue, in the nation is between the University of Louisville Cardinals and the University of Kentucky Wildcats. Separated by a mere 78 miles, the universities first met on the gridiron in 1912. Since 1994 the schools have competed annually in football for The Governor's Cup, a trophy awarded to the winning team. Whether you bleed red or blue, football season wouldn't be complete without a tailgating party (or two!)

TOUCHDOWN CRUNCH SLAW

1/2 cup buttermilk
2 tablespoons mayonnaise
2 tablespoons sour cream
2 tablespoons cider vinegar
2 tablespoons minced shallots
1 tablespoon sugar
1/2 teaspoon salt
1/4 teaspoon pepper
3 tablespoons chopped chives
1 pound napa cabbage, shredded
6 radishes, chopped
2 ribs celery, thinly sliced diagonally
2 Granny Smith apples, chopped
1/2 cup crumbled blue cheese

Serves 8

Whisk the buttermilk, mayonnaise, sour cream, vinegar, shallots, sugar, salt and pepper in a large bowl. Whisk in the chives. Add the cabbage, radishes, celery and apples and toss to mix. Sprinkle with the blue cheese.

SWEET POTATO SALAD

1/2 cup extra-virgin olive oil
3/4 teaspoon herbes de Provence
1/4 teaspoon sea salt
1/8 teaspoon black pepper
6 1/2 pounds sweet potatoes, peeled and
   cut into 1/2-inch slices
3 tablespoons fresh lime juice
2 garlic cloves, crushed to a paste
1/2 teaspoon cumin
1/8 teaspoon red pepper flakes
4 piquillo peppers, finely chopped
2/3 cup finely chopped celery
4 scallions, sliced
2 tablespoons chopped fresh cilantro

Serves 6

Whisk the olive oil, herbes de Provence, salt and black pepper in a large bowl. Add the potatoes and toss to coat. Remove the potatoes and arrange in a single layer in a shallow baking pan. Reserve the oil mixture. Bake the potatoes in a preheated 450-degree oven for 8 to 10 minutes. Remove to a wire rack to cool completely. Chop the potatoes. Whisk the lime juice, garlic, cumin and red pepper flakes into the reserved oil mixture. Add the potatoes, peppers, celery, scallions and cilantro and mix gently. Chill until ready to serve; the flavors enhance with time. Bring to room temperature before serving.

Chef: Chef Ghyslain Maurais, Ghyslain

UK vs. UofL Governor's Cup Cupcakes

Cupcakes

2 1/2 cups cake flour
1 teaspoon salt
1 cup (2 sticks) butter, softened
2 cups sugar
2 eggs
1 cup buttermilk
1 teaspoon vanilla extract
1/2 teaspoon baking soda
1 tablespoon white vinegar
1 tablespoon baking cocoa
1 1/2 tablespoons red or blue liquid
   food coloring
1 drop violet gel food coloring
   (optional—for blue cupcakes)
Red or blue sprinkles (optional)

Serves 24

Cream Cheese Frosting

16 ounces cream cheese, softened
1 cup (2 sticks) butter, softened
1 teaspoon vanilla extract
4 cups sifted confectioners' sugar

Makes 4 cups

*M*ix the cake flour and salt together. Beat the butter and sugar in a mixing bowl until light and fluffy. Add the eggs one at a time, beating well after each addition. Beat in the flour mixture 1/2 cup at a time, alternating with the buttermilk. Beat in the vanilla. Mix the baking soda and vinegar in a small bowl. Beat into the batter. Mix the baking cocoa, liquid food coloring and gel food coloring to a paste in a small bowl. Beat into the batter.

Fill paper-lined muffin cups two-thirds full. Bake in a preheated 350-degree oven for 25 to 30 minutes or until a wooden pick inserted in the center comes out clean. Remove to a wire rack to cool completely. Frost when cool and top with sprinkles.

Note: You must use cake flour in this recipe. All-purpose flour will give the cupcakes a totally different texture. While these are ideal for the UK vs. UofL rivalry, they also make great Fourth of July cupcakes, too!

*B*eat the cream cheese, butter and vanilla in a mixing bowl until smooth. Beat in the confectioners' sugar gradually at low speed. Increase the speed to high and beat for 2 minutes or until light and fluffy.

St. James Court Art Show

Serves 8

BRUNCH

ST. JAMES COURT ART SHOW STRATA

BLUEGRASS BOURBON MAPLE BACON

FINE ART FRIED BISCUITS WITH MAPLE PUMPKIN BUTTER

LUNCH

APPLE PARSNIP SOUP

KFC RED CURRY GRILLED CHICKEN SALAD

BELGRAVIA COURT BRUSSELS SPROUT SALAD

TURKEY CRANBERRY SANDWICH

CRANBERRY RELISH

ARTFULLY INSPIRED EVERYTHING OATMEAL COOKIES

KENTUCKY MIMOSA

St. James Court Art Show Menu Sponsored by

Jamie Estes, Estes Public Relations

ESTES

PUBLIC
RELATIONS

Belgravia Court Brussels Sprout Salad

ST. JAMES COURT ART SHOW STRATA

5 large plum tomatoes
1 teaspoon kosher salt
1 (1-pound) loaf Italian bread, trimmed and
    cut into 1/2-inch-thick slices
4 ounces herbed goat cheese, softened
1 1/2 cups (6 ounces) shredded white
    Cheddar cheese
8 eggs
4 cups milk
2 tablespoons Dijon mustard
1 teaspoon kosher salt
1/4 teaspoon freshly ground pepper
1 tablespoon chopped basil

Serves 12

Cut the tomatoes into 1/2-inch slices and
remove the seeds. Arrange in a large colander
and sprinkle with 1 teaspoon salt. Let drain for
30 minutes. Remove the tomato slices to paper
towels and pat dry.

Arrange half the bread slices in the bottom
of a greased 9×13-inch baking dish. Spread the
bread with half the goat cheese and sprinkle with
half the Cheddar cheese. Repeat the layers and
arrange the tomato slices over the top.

Whisk the eggs, milk, Dijon mustard,
1 teaspoon salt and the pepper in a bowl. Pour
evenly over the bread mixture. Chill, covered,
overnight. Remove the strata from the refrigerator
and let stand for 30 minutes.

Bake, uncovered, in a preheated 350-degree
oven for 60 to 70 minutes or until a knife inserted
in the center comes out clean. Let stand for
20 minutes. Sprinkle with the basil and serve.

BLUEGRASS BOURBON MAPLE BACON

1/2 cup maple syrup
1 tablespoon Kentucky bourbon
2 pounds thick cut bacon

Serves 6 to 8

Mix the maple syrup and bourbon in a bowl.
Line a shallow baking pan with foil or baking
parchment. Place a stainless steel baking rack in
the pan. Arrange the bacon slices on the rack in a
single layer. Brush the bacon with the maple
syrup mixture. Bake in a preheated 375-degree
oven for 15 to 20 minutes or until the bacon begins
to brown. Brush the bacon with the maple syrup
mixture again and bake for 3 to 5 minutes longer.

FINE ART FRIED BISCUITS WITH MAPLE PUMPKIN BUTTER

BISCUITS

2 cups all-purpose flour
1 tablespoon baking powder
1/2 teaspoon salt
3 tablespoons sugar
3/4 cup milk
2 cups (about) vegetable oil

Serves 12

MAPLE PUMPKIN BUTTER

3 1/2 cups pumpkin purée
3/4 cup packed light brown sugar
1/2 cup maple syrup
Zest of 1 large lemon
2 tablespoons lemon juice
1 teaspoon cinnamon
1 teaspoon ginger
1/2 teaspoon ground nutmeg
1/4 teaspoon cardamom
1/8 teaspoon ground cloves
1/2 teaspoon salt
1 teaspoon vanilla extract

Makes 2 1/2 to 3 cups

Whisk the flour, baking powder, salt and sugar in a bowl. Add the milk and stir to combine. Divide the dough into two balls. Knead each ball a few times on a floured surface. Pat out each to a 1/2-inch-thick circle and cut with a 2-inch biscuit cutter. Add the oil to a depth of 1/2 inch in a heavy skillet and heat over medium-high heat until hot. Fry the biscuits in batches until golden brown on both sides. Remove to paper towels to drain. Serve warm with maple pumpkin butter.

Mix the pumpkin, brown sugar, maple syrup, lemon zest, lemon juice, cinnamon, ginger, nutmeg, cardamom, cloves and salt in a saucepan. Simmer for 20 to 30 minutes, stirring occasionally near the beginning and more frequently the last 15 minutes of cooking. Cook until the mixture is thickened and reduced to 2 1/2 to 3 cups and is a silky, spreadable consistency. Remove from the heat and stir in the vanilla. Cool completely and spoon into a sealable container. Chill until ready to use.

Note: If the pumpkin butter is too thick after chilling, thin with a little water or apple juice.

*C*apriole Farmstead in Greenville, Indiana, makes fresh, ripened, and aged chevres by hand, using only the milk of their own herd. Make the St. James Court Art Show Strata (page 120) extra special by using this exquisite local goat cheese.

APPLE PARSNIP SOUP

2 tablespoons olive oil
1 cup chopped onion
2¹/₂ cups chopped peeled Pink Lady apples
1 tablespoon curry powder
¹/₂ teaspoon grated fresh ginger
1 teaspoon ground cardamom
1 garlic clove, chopped
3¹/₂ cups chopped peeled parsnips
4 cups chicken broth
1 cup apple cider
¹/₂ teaspoon salt
¹/₈ teaspoon freshly ground pepper
8 teaspoons crème fraîche
¹/₂ cup toasted pumpkin seeds

Serves 8

*H*eat the olive oil in a heavy saucepan over medium heat. Add the onion and sauté for 5 minutes or until tender. Add the apples, curry powder, ginger, cardamom and garlic and sauté for 1 minute. Stir in the parsnips, broth and apple cider. Bring to a boil. Reduce the heat and simmer, covered, for 30 minutes or until the parsnips are tender. Remove from the heat. Purée the soup with an immersion blender or in batches in a countertop blender. Remove to a bowl and stir in the salt and pepper. Ladle the soup into eight serving bowls and top each with 1 teaspoon crème fraîche and 1 tablespoon pumpkin seeds.

KFC RED CURRY GRILLED CHICKEN SALAD

1 tablespoon peanut oil
2 teaspoons red curry paste
4 KFC grilled boneless chicken breasts,
    finely chopped
¹/₂ cup canned coconut milk
1 teaspoon fish sauce
1 tablespoon honey
1 kaffir lime leaf, minced
6 Thai basil leaves, coarsely chopped
2 tablespoons minced green bell pepper
2 tablespoons minced celery
1 tablespoon minced water chestnuts
2 tablespoons dry roasted peanuts, chopped

Serves 8 to 12

*H*eat the peanut oil in a skillet over medium-high heat for 45 seconds. Add the curry paste and sauté for 1 minute. Add the chicken and remove from the heat. Mix well and let cool completely. Mix the coconut milk, fish sauce and honey in a large bowl. Fold in the chicken mixture, lime leaf, basil, bell pepper, celery, water chestnuts and peanuts. Chill for at least 1 hour. Serve with fried won ton chips.

Note: Recipe compliments of KFC.

BELGRAVIA COURT BRUSSELS SPROUT SALAD

SALAD

2 pounds large brussels sprouts, trimmed and
    cut into halves lengthwise
2 cups (1-inch) butternut squash chunks
1/3 cup olive oil
1 teaspoon salt
1/2 teaspoon pepper
1/2 cup thinly sliced green onions
1/4 cup chopped flat-leaf parsley

Serves 10

CHAMPAGNE VINAIGRETTE

1 tablespoon Dijon mustard
1 large garlic clove, minced
2 1/2 tablespoons Champagne vinegar
1/2 teaspoon sugar
1/2 teaspoon salt
1/4 teaspoon pepper
1/2 cup extra-virgin olive oil

Makes 3/4 cup

Combine the brussels sprouts, squash, olive oil, salt and pepper in a large bowl and toss to coat. Spread in a single layer on 1 or 2 large baking sheets. Roast in a preheated 450-degree oven for 20 to 30 minutes or until brown, turning the vegetables over halfway through roasting and reversing the pan placement. Remove the vegetables to a bowl and let cool to warm. Add the green onions and parsley and toss to mix. Add desired amount of Champagne vinaigrette and toss to coat. Serve warm or at room temperature.

Whisk the Dijon mustard, garlic, vinegar, sugar, salt and pepper in a bowl. Whisk in the olive oil slowly.

The St. James Court Art Show is a nationally acclaimed annual event that takes place on the streets of Old Louisville the first weekend of October. The St. James Court Art Show debuted in 1957 with fifteen exhibitors in the hopes of raising funds to repair the iconic St. James Court Fountain. Today nearly 750 exhibitors showcase their paintings, textiles, photography, and other artistic talent to more than 300,000 attendees. Whether you invite your friends over before heading to the festival for breakfast, or after you visit the festival for lunch, this menu is sure to please.

Turkey Cranberry Sandwich

Herb-Roasted Turkey

3 tablespoons olive oil
3/4 teaspoon chopped fresh rosemary
3/4 teaspoon chopped fresh sage
3/4 teaspoon chopped fresh parsley
3/4 teaspoon chopped fresh thyme
3/4 teaspoon kosher salt
3/4 teaspoon freshly ground pepper
1 (6-pound) bone-in turkey breast
1 cup dry white wine

Serves 4 to 6

*W*hisk the olive oil, rosemary, sage, parsley, thyme, salt and pepper in a small bowl. Place the turkey breast side up in a roasting pan coated with nonstick cooking spray. Rub the herb mixture over the turkey. Pour the wine into the bottom of the pan. Roast, loosely covered with foil, in a preheated 325-degree oven for 2 hours. Remove the foil and roast for 30 minutes longer or until the turkey is cooked through. Remove to a wire rack and let stand for 45 minutes before carving. The turkey can be made up to 2 days ahead and refrigerated until ready to serve.

Sandwich

1/2 cup Dijon mustard
8 to 12 slices good-quality multigrain bread
12 ounces brie cheese, sliced
2 cups Cranberry Relish (page 125)
1 cup baby arugula
1/2 to 3/4 cup (1 to 1 1/2 sticks) butter

Serves 4 to 6

*S*lice 3 pounds of the turkey. Spread the Dijon mustard over half the bread slices. Top with the turkey and cheese. Spread the cranberry relish over the cheese and top with the arugula. Top with the remaining bread slices. Melt 1 tablespoon of the butter in a nonstick skillet over medium-high heat. Add one sandwich and cook until the cheese starts to melt and the bottom of the bread is golden brown. Add 1 tablespoon butter to the skillet and turn the sandwich over. Cook until the bottom of the bread is golden brown. Repeat with the remaining sandwiches.

Kentucky Mimosa

3/4 ounce Kentucky bourbon
1 ounce sparkling apple cider
Ginger ale

Serves 1

*P*our the bourbon and cider into a Champagne flute. Fill to the top with ginger ale.

Note: Recipe compliments of Joy Perrine, Jack's Lounge

CRANBERRY RELISH

2 cups fresh cranberries
1 cup raisins (optional)
1 cup sugar
1/2 tablespoon grated orange zest
1/2 cup orange juice
1 slightly underripe pear or ripe apple,
    peeled and sliced
1 cinnamon stick
1/8 teaspoon each ground allspice, cardamom
    and cloves
2 tablespoons Kentucky bourbon

Makes 2 cups

Mix all the ingredients in a heavy saucepan. Cook over medium heat for 10 minutes or until the cranberries pop, stirring frequently. Press the cranberries against the side of the pan to be certain they pop. Reduce the heat to low and simmer for 45 to 60 minutes, stirring occasionally. Skim off any foam and remove the cinnamon stick. Remove the relish to a bowl and cool.

Note: This relish keeps for up to 2 months in a sealed container in the refrigerator.

ARTFULLY INSPIRED EVERYTHING OATMEAL COOKIES

1 1/2 cups all-purpose flour
3/4 cup packed brown sugar
1 teaspoon baking soda
1/2 teaspoon salt
3 cups rolled oats
1 cup chopped dried cherries
1/4 cup flaked coconut, toasted
1/2 cup (1 stick) butter, softened
1/2 cup granulated sugar
2 eggs
1 teaspoon vanilla extract
1/2 cup white chocolate chips
1/4 cup macadamia nuts, chopped

Makes 3 dozen

Mix the flour, brown sugar, baking soda and salt in a bowl. Stir in the oats, cherries and coconut. Beat the butter, granulated sugar, eggs and vanilla in a mixing bowl until light and fluffy. Beat in the oat mixture 1/2 cup at a time on medium speed. Fold in the white chocolate chips and nuts. Drop by large spoonfuls onto greased cookie sheets. Bake in a preheated 350-degree oven for 8 to 10 minutes or until the bottoms are golden brown and the cookies are still soft. Cool on the cookie sheet for 2 minutes. Remove to a wire rack to cool completely.

Variation: Feel free to substitute your favorite dried fruit for the dried cherries.

Oktoberfest

Serves 8

Beer Cheese

Laugen Brz'n Pretzel Bread

Barrett Avenue Beer Beef Soup

Schnitzelburg Slaw

Warm Germantown Potato Salad

German Chocolate Harvest Moon Pies

German Chocolate Harvest Moon Pies

BEER CHEESE

1/2 cup (1 stick) butter
1 cup all-purpose flour
1 cup lager
1 cup cream
8 ounces Gouda cheese, shredded
Salt to taste

Serves 12

Melt the butter in a saucepan over low heat. Whisk in the flour. Cook for 3 to 5 minutes, stirring constantly. Mix the beer and cream in a stainless steel saucepan. Bring to a boil over medium heat. Whisk into the flour mixture 1 teaspoon at a time and cook to desired thickness, whisking constantly. Remove from the heat. Add the cheese, a small amount at a time, stirring until the cheese is melted before adding more cheese. Season with salt and pour into a serving bowl. Serve with baguette slices for dipping.

Note: If the dip seems too thick, thin with a small amount of beer or cream.

Chef: Chef Brian Morgan, Eiderdown

Every fall, Louisville's German community celebrates Oktoberfest, a scaled down version of the sixteen-day German festival that lasts two days and focuses on merriment and the consumption of beer. The Germans first settled in Louisville in 1787, establishing, among other things, many of the meat-packing companies and dairy operations in the neighborhoods of Butchertown and Germantown. Today, still roughly a third of the city's population can trace their ancestry back to their German roots. Celebrate our German roots with a beer in one hand and a brat in the other.

LAUGEN BRZ'N PRETZEL BREAD

4 teaspoons dry yeast
1 teaspoon sugar
1 1/4 cups warm water (110 degrees)
5 cups all-purpose flour
1/2 cup sugar
1 1/2 teaspoons salt
1 tablespoon vegetable oil
1/2 cup baking soda
4 cups hot water
1/4 cup kosher salt
1/2 cup (1 stick) butter or margarine, melted

Serves 12

Dissolve the yeast and 1 teaspoon sugar in 1 1/4 cups warm water in a bowl. Let stand for 10 minutes. Mix the flour, 1/2 cup sugar and 1 1/2 teaspoons salt in a large bowl. Make a well in the center of the flour mixture. Pour the yeast mixture and oil into the well and stir to make a dough. Add 1 to 2 tablespoons of water if the dough is too dry. Knead the dough on a floured surface for 7 to 8 minutes or until smooth. Place the dough in an oiled bowl and turn to coat. Cover with plastic wrap and let rise in a warm place for 1 hour or until doubled in bulk.

Remove the dough to a floured surface and divide into 24 equal pieces. Roll each piece into a 10- to 12-inch rod. Dissolve the baking soda in 4 cups hot water in a bowl. Dip each rod into the baking soda mixture and arrange on a greased baking sheet. Sprinkle the rods with the kosher salt. Bake in a preheated 450-degree oven for 8 minutes or until golden brown. Remove to a wire rack and brush the pretzel rods with the melted butter.

Variation: If a pretzel shape is desired, divide the dough into 12 equal pieces and roll each piece into a 20- to 24-inch rope. Shape each rope into a pretzel and follow the remaining instructions.

BARRETT AVENUE BEER BEEF SOUP

1 tablespoon olive oil
1 pound lean ground beef
1 onion, chopped
3 ribs celery, chopped
6 tomatoes, chopped
1/2 head cabbage, coarsely chopped
4 (14-ounce) cans beef broth
1 (15-ounce) can black beans
1 (15-ounce) can red kidney beans
2 cups water
1 (12-ounce) can beer
1 cup barley
1/2 teaspoon hickory liquid smoke
Salt and pepper to taste

Serves 8 to 10

Heat the olive oil in a large saucepan. Add the ground beef and cook until crumbly; drain. Add the onion and celery and sauté until the onion is translucent. Add the tomatoes and cabbage and sauté until the cabbage is wilted.

Stir in the broth, black beans, kidney beans, water and beer. Bring to a boil and stir in the barley. Reduce the heat and simmer for 30 minutes or until the barley is tender. Stir in the liquid smoke. Simmer for 10 to 15 minutes. Season with salt and pepper and serve.

Variation: You may substitute 1 (28-ounce) can diced tomatoes for the fresh tomatoes. If you would like some heat, add 1 chopped dried cayenne pepper.

When it comes to good beer, it's not hard to find in Kentucky. Brewing in the River City goes back to the early 1900s. Building on this foundation, microbreweries and brewpubs are popping up all over the state. Many of these breweries offer tastings and trainings and also participate in multiple local and regional craft beer festivals. If you're from out of town, are new to the city, or have never tried craft beer, be sure to stop by one of our local breweries or attend one of the many festivals. You might just find a new hobby—home brewing is also on the rise!

Schnitzelburg Slaw

3 cups thinly sliced red cabbage
   (about 1/2 head cabbage)
1/2 cup chopped fresh parsley
1/2 cup shredded carrots
2 fennel bulbs, trimmed and thinly sliced
Salt and pepper to taste
Fennel fronds for garnish

Serves 8

Orange Dressing

1/2 cup orange juice
1/2 cup olive oil
1/4 cup cider vinegar
2 tablespoons honey
1 tablespoon sugar

Makes 1 1/3 cups

*C*ombine the cabbage, parsley, carrots and sliced fennel in a large bowl and toss to mix. Add the desired amount of orange dressing and toss to coat. Season with salt and pepper and chill until ready to serve. Garnish with fennel fronds before serving.

*W*hisk the orange juice, olive oil, vinegar, honey and sugar in a bowl or in a container with a tight-fitting lid and shake well.

Note: The dressing for this slaw also makes a tasty salad dressing. Pour over fresh baby spinach, sliced red onion, mandarin oranges and almonds to create a quick and delicious salad.

WARM GERMANTOWN POTATO SALAD

6 red potatoes
1 tablespoon canola oil or olive oil
3/4 cup chopped yellow onion
1 tablespoon all-purpose flour
1 1/2 tablespoons sugar
1/2 teaspoon salt
1/2 teaspoon pepper
1/2 teaspoon celery seeds
3/4 cup water
1/3 cup cider vinegar
2 teaspoons Dijon mustard
3 slices bacon, crisp-cooked and crumbled
2 tablespoons chopped fresh parsley

Serves 8

Place the potatoes in a 4-quart saucepan. Add water just to cover. Bring to a boil and then reduce the heat to low. Simmer, covered, for 25 to 30 minutes or until the potatoes are tender; drain. Cool the potatoes slightly and cut into slices.

Heat the canola oil in a nonstick skillet over medium heat. Add the onion and sauté for 3 to 4 minutes or until tender. Stir in the flour, sugar, salt, pepper and celery seeds and cook for 2 minutes, stirring constantly. Stir in the water, vinegar and Dijon mustard gradually. Cook for 2 to 3 minutes or until bubbly and thickened, stirring constantly. Add the potatoes and bacon. Cook until heated through, stirring frequently. Sprinkle with the parsley and serve.

Variation: For added heat, use a spicy Dijon mustard.

Round out this menu by serving up a brat bar. Boil bratwursts in beer and let your guests choose from an array of toppings. Include items such as sauerkraut, Swiss cheese, sautéed onions and peppers, mustard, ketchup, pickle relish, and jalapeño chiles...and don't forget the buns!

132

GERMAN CHOCOLATE HARVEST MOON PIES

GERMAN CHOCOLATE COOKIES

2 cups all-purpose flour
5 tablespoons baking cocoa
1 1/8 teaspoons baking powder
1 teaspoon baking soda
1/2 cup shortening or softened
    unsalted butter
1 cup sugar
2 egg yolks
1 teaspoon vanilla extract
1 cup milk

Serves 15

*S*ift the flour, baking cocoa, baking powder and baking soda together. Beat the shortening, sugar, egg yolks and vanilla in a mixing bowl for 2 minutes. Beat in the dry ingredients alternately with the whole milk, beginning and ending with the dry ingredients. Drop by very rounded tablespoonfuls 3 inches apart onto a 10×15-inch cookie sheet lined with baking parchment. Bake in a preheated 375-degree oven for 8 to 10 minutes or until the cookies are slightly puffed and still soft. Cool on the cookie sheet for 10 minutes. Remove to a wire rack to cool completely.

Spread equal portions of the Coconut Pecan Filling over the flat side of half the cookies. Top with the remaining cookies, flat side down.

Note: These cookies can be made 1 day ahead and stored in an airtight container.

COCONUT PECAN FILLING

3/4 cup evaporated milk
3/4 cup sugar
6 tablespoons unsalted butter
3 egg yolks, lightly beaten
1 cup sweetened flaked coconut
3/4 teaspoon vanilla extract
1 cup chopped pecans, toasted

Makes 3 1/2 cups

*C*ombine the evaporated milk, sugar, butter and egg yolks in a heavy 3-quart saucepan. Cook over medium heat for 12 to 14 minutes or to a light caramel color and a pudding consistency, stirring constantly. Remove from the heat and stir in the coconut, vanilla and pecans. Remove to a bowl and let stand for 45 minutes or until cool, stirring occasionally.

Breeders' Cup Brunch

Serves 6

OPENING CEREMONY GRAND ORANGES

PEAR AND BLUE CHEESE SALAD WITH CRANBERRY VINAIGRETTE

THOROUGHBRED HOT BROWN TART

BROCCOLI AND CAULIFLOWER GRATIN

PADDOCK PESTO SCONES

KENTUCKY JAM CAKE

CRANBERRY PECAN BARS

VINT JULEP

DOWN THE STRETCH

Breeders' Cup Brunch Menu Sponsored by

M. A. BUCKNER

Thoroughbred Hot Brown Tart

OPENING CEREMONY GRAND ORANGES

1/4 cup sugar
1 (6-ounce) jar orange marmalade
1/2 tablespoon grated fresh ginger
2 tablespoons orange liqueur
8 large oranges, peeled and sectioned
2 tablespoons finely chopped fresh mint
Orange zest strips for garnish

Serves 6

Cook the sugar, marmalade and ginger in a small saucepan over medium heat until the sugar is dissolved, stirring constantly. Remove to a bowl and cool slightly. Stir in the liqueur and oranges. Chill, covered, for 8 hours. Sprinkle with the mint and garnish with orange zest strips.

VINT JULEP

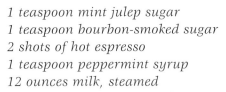

1 teaspoon mint julep sugar
1 teaspoon bourbon-smoked sugar
2 shots of hot espresso
1 teaspoon peppermint syrup
12 ounces milk, steamed
Whipped cream for garnish

Serves 1

Combine the sugars and espresso in a cup. Stir in the syrup. Top with steamed milk and garnish with whipped cream.

Note: Recipe compliments of Toni Lavenson, VINT Coffee

The Breeders' Cup World Championships, commonly known as the "richest day in sports," is a two-day annual event that takes place in November. It attracts the top thoroughbred race horses from around the world. While the event's location has typically changed each year, the legendary Churchill Downs in south Louisville has hosted the Breeders' Cup more than any other track in the country. Regardless of the location, celebrate this day Kentucky-style with a Hot Brown Tart (page 138) and Jam Cake (page 140)!

PEAR AND BLUE CHEESE SALAD WITH CRANBERRY VINAIGRETTE

2 egg whites
1 1/2 cups packed brown sugar
1 1/2 teaspoons salt
1 1/2 cups coarsely chopped walnuts
18 leaves of Boston lettuce
   (about 2 heads lettuce)
2 cups sliced peeled pears (about 2 pears)
1 cup thinly sliced red onion, separated
   into rings
1/3 cup (2 ounces) crumbled blue cheese

Serves 6

CRANBERRY VINAIGRETTE

1 1/2 cups cranberry juice cocktail
3/4 cup sweetened dried cranberries
1/4 cup red wine vinegar
3 tablespoons finely chopped shallots
1 teaspoon minced fresh ginger
2 tablespoons hazelnut oil or olive oil
1/4 teaspoon kosher salt
1/4 teaspoon freshly ground pepper

Makes 2 1/2 cups

*S*tir the egg whites gently in a bowl for 30 seconds. Add the brown sugar and salt and mix well. Add the walnuts and stir well to coat. Spread the walnuts evenly on a baking sheet coated with nonstick cooking spray. Bake in a preheated 300-degree oven for 15 to 20 minutes or to a medium brown color. Rotate the pan halfway through baking; do not stir. Remove to a wire rack to cool. Break into pieces when cool.

Divide the lettuce among six salad plates and top with equal portions of the pears and onion. Drizzle with cranberry vinaigrette and sprinkle with equal portions of the cheese and candied walnuts.

*B*ring the cranberry juice cocktail and cranberries to a boil in a small saucepan. Reduce the heat and simmer for 10 minutes or until the liquid is reduced by half. Remove from the heat and stir in the vinegar, shallots and ginger. Purée the mixture with an immersion blender or in a countertop blender. Add the hazelnut oil in a slow stream while blending. Pour into a bowl and stir in the salt and pepper. Cool to room temperature before using.

THOROUGHBRED HOT BROWN TART

2 refrigerated pie pastries
1 1/2 cups chopped cooked turkey
2 cups (8 ounces) shredded Gruyère cheese
1/4 cup finely chopped green onions,
   including dark green part
6 slices bacon, crisp-cooked and crumbled
4 eggs
1 1/2 cups half-and-half
1/2 teaspoon salt
1/4 teaspoon freshly ground pepper
2 plum tomatoes, cut into 1/4-inch slices
1/2 cup (2 ounces) freshly grated Parmesan
   cheese

Serves 6 to 8

Unroll the pie pastries and stack together. Fit the pastries into a 10-inch deep-dish tart pan with a removable bottom, pressing the pastry into the fluted edge. Trim the edge. Line with foil or baking parchment Place pie weights or dried beans in the pastry shell. Bake on a baking sheet in a preheated 425-degree oven for 12 minutes. Remove the foil and weights; bake for 8 minutes longer. Remove to a wire rack to cool complete. Reduce the oven temperature to 350 degrees.

Layer the turkey, Gruyère cheese, green onions and bacon in the cooled crust. Whisk the eggs, half-and-half, salt and pepper in a bowl. Pour over the turkey mixture. Bake at 350 degrees for 30 to 40 minutes or until set.

Lay the tomato slices on paper towels and press lightly with paper towels to remove excess moisture. Arrange the tomato slices over the top of the tart and sprinkle with the Parmesan cheese. Bake at 350 degrees for 10 to 15 minutes or until the cheese is melted. Cool on the baking sheet for 15 minutes. Run a sharp knife around the edge of the tart and remove the side of the pan.

DOWN THE STRETCH

1 1/2 parts vodka
1/2 part blue curaçao
1 part lemon-lime soda
1 part cranberry juice
1 part sweet-and-sour mix
Blackberries and lemon slices for garnish

Serves a variable amount

Combine the vodka, liqueur, lemon-lime soda, cranberry juice and sweet-and-sour mix in a cocktail shaker or tall glass filled with ice. Shake or stir vigorously and serve over ice. Garnish each serving with a fresh blackberry and a slice of lemon.

Note: This is the signature drink of the Breeders' Cup World Championships.

BROCCOLI AND CAULIFLOWER GRATIN

3 cups chopped fresh cauliflower
3 cups chopped fresh broccoli
Salt to taste
1/4 cup (1/2 stick) unsalted butter
1/4 cup all-purpose flour
1 1/2 cups milk
1 garlic clove, minced
1 teaspoon red pepper flakes
1 cup (4 ounces) grated Parmesan and
    pecorino cheese blend
1/4 teaspoon salt
1/4 teaspoon freshly ground pepper
1/8 teaspoon ground nutmeg
1/2 cup plain bread crumbs or panko

Serves 6

*B*lanch the cauliflower and broccoli in a large saucepan of boiling salted water for 1 to 2 minutes; drain. Spoon into a greased 9×13-inch baking dish. Let cool for 5 minutes. Melt the butter in a saucepan over medium heat. Whisk in the flour and cook for 2 minutes, whisking constantly. Whisk in the milk slowly. Reduce the heat to low and stir in the garlic and red pepper flakes. Cook until the mixture coats the back of a spoon, stirring constantly. Stir in the cheese, salt, pepper and nutmeg. Pour evenly over the vegetables in the baking dish and top with the bread crumbs. Bake in a preheated 350-degree oven for 25 minutes or until the bread crumbs are golden brown. Serve immediately.

Variation: Top the bread crumbs with crisp-cooked pancetta before baking.

PADDOCK PESTO SCONES

3 1/4 cups all-purpose flour
1 tablespoon sugar
2 1/2 teaspoons baking powder
1/2 teaspoon baking soda
3/4 teaspoon salt
1/4 teaspoon pepper
3/4 cup (1 1/2 sticks) cold butter, cut into pieces
1 cup plain yogurt
1/4 cup pesto
2/3 cup grated pecorino Romano cheese
Grated zest of 1 lemon
Melted butter

Makes 12 to 16

*M*ix the flour, sugar, baking powder, baking soda, salt and pepper in a bowl. Cut in the cold butter with a pastry blender, fork or clean hands until crumbly. Add the yogurt, pesto, cheese and lemon zest and stir until a dough forms. Bring the dough together with clean hands and turn out onto a floured surface. Knead the dough gently. Divide the dough in half and pat each half into a circle. Cut each circle into 6 to 8 wedges using a pizza cutter. Arrange the wedges on a nonstick baking sheet and brush with melted butter. Bake in a preheated 425-degree oven for 12 to 14 minutes. Remove to a wire rack to cool.

KENTUCKY JAM CAKE

CAKE

4 cups all-purpose flour
1/2 teaspoon salt
1 teaspoon allspice
1 teaspoon cinnamon
1/2 teaspoon ground cloves
1/2 teaspoon nutmeg
1 cup buttermilk, at room temperature
2 teaspoons baking soda
1 cup (2 sticks) butter, softened
2 cups sugar
1 teaspoon vanilla extract
5 eggs, at room temperature
1 cup raisins or favorite dried fruit
1/2 cup chopped walnuts
1/2 cup chopped pecans
2 cups blackberry jam
Pecan halves and candied cherries
   for garnish

Serves 16 or more

Variation: You may substitute any flavor
of dark jam or combination of jams for the
blackberry jam.

Sift the flour, salt, allspice, cinnamon, cloves
and nutmeg together. Mix the buttermilk and
baking soda in a bowl. Beat the butter, sugar and
vanilla in a mixing bowl until light and fluffy.
Add the eggs one at a time, beating well after
each addition. Add the dry ingredients alternately
with the buttermilk, beating well after each
addition. Beat in the raisins, walnuts, chopped
pecans and jam. Divide the batter between a
greased and floured bundt pan and a greased and
floured loaf pan. Bake in a preheated 350-degree
oven for 40 to 45 minutes for the loaf pan and
50 to 60 minutes for the bundt pan or until a
wooden pick inserted in the center comes out
clean. Remove to a wire rack to cool completely.

Invert the cooled cakes onto serving platters.
Drizzle the caramel sauce over the cakes. Store
in sealed containers for 2 or 3 days. Garnish
with pecans and candied cherries. Slice thinly
and serve.

Note: The loaf cake makes a great hostess
gift. Wrap in butcher's paper and tie with a
festive ribbon.

*Jam cakes are a Kentucky holiday tradition. Take advantage of all the delicious nuts
and preserved fruit available during the holidays. This cake is sure to make your
house smell like the holidays!*

CARAMEL SAUCE

2 1/4 cups packed light brown sugar
10 tablespoons butter
1 1/2 cups (or more) cream or evaporated milk
2 1/4 cups confectioners' sugar, sifted
1 1/2 teaspoons vanilla extract

Serves 25

Combine the brown sugar, butter and 1 1/2 cups cream in a heavy saucepan. Bring to a boil and cook for 2 minutes, stirring frequently. Remove from the heat and let cool for 5 minutes. Beat in the confectioners' sugar and vanilla. If the sauce is too thick, beat in additional cream, 1 tablespoon at a time, until of the desired consistency

Note: If you have caramel sauce leftover, use it on ice cream, coffee cake, bread pudding or any of your favorite sweet treats.

CRANBERRY PECAN BARS

1 cup all-purpose flour
2 tablespoons sugar
1/3 cup butter, softened
1/2 cup finely chopped pecans
1 1/4 cups sugar
2 tablespoons all-purpose flour
2 eggs, beaten
2 tablespoons milk
1 tablespoon grated orange zest
1 teaspoon vanilla extract
1 cup chopped fresh or frozen cranberries
1/2 cup flaked coconut
1/2 cup finely chopped pecans

Makes 3 dozen

Mix 1 cup flour and 2 tablespoons sugar in a bowl. Cut in the butter with a pastry blender until crumbly. Stir in 1/2 cup pecans. Press over the bottom of an ungreased 9×13-inch baking pan. Bake in a preheated 350-degree oven for 15 to 20 minutes. Maintain the oven temperature.

Combine 1 1/4 cups sugar and 2 tablespoons flour in a bowl. Stir in the eggs, milk, orange zest and vanilla. Fold in the cranberries, coconut and 1/2 cup pecans. Spread over the crust. Bake for 25 to 35 minutes or until the top is golden brown. Remove to a wire rack and cut into bars. Cool completely before removing the bars from the pan.

Note: These bars freeze well and are nice for gift-giving.

Harvest Dinner

Serves 6

Beet Salad with Pistachios and Goat Cheese

Rosemary and Sage White Bean Spread

Autumn Roasted Chicken

Harvest Stuffed Sugar Pumpkin

Savory Roasted Root Vegetables

Tok-Sel Lima Beans

White Chocolate Bread Pudding with
Tart Cherries and Caramel

Maple Bourbon Cider

Harvest Dinner Menu Sponsored by

Kentucky Proud

Harvest Stuffed Sugar Pumpkin

BEET SALAD WITH PISTACHIOS AND GOAT CHEESE

Kosher salt
3 large red beets, trimmed
2 large yellow beets, trimmed
1/4 cup minced shallot
2 tablespoons fresh lemon juice
3/4 teaspoon kosher salt
1/4 teaspoon freshly ground pepper
1/4 cup olive oil
4 ounces goat cheese, crumbled
2 tablespoons shelled pistachios, chopped
2 cups frisée
1 cup fresh spinach

Serves 6 to 8

Cover the bottom of a 9×13-inch baking pan with kosher salt. Arrange the beets in the pan by color, making certain the beets don't touch. Cover the pan tightly with foil. Roast in a preheated 425-degree oven for 1 to 1 1/2 hours or until tender. Remove to a wire rack to cool.

Slip the skins off the beets when cool enough to handle. Cut the beets into 1/4-inch pieces and place the red beets in one bowl and the yellow beets in another bowl.

Whisk the shallot, lemon juice, 3/4 teaspoon salt and the pepper in a bowl. Whisk in the olive oil in a steady stream. Add 2 1/2 tablespoons of the dressing to each bowl of beets and toss to mix.

For each serving, place a round cookie cutter in the center of a salad plate. Spoon equal portions of the red beets into the cookie cutter and press down gently. Crumble 2 teaspoons of the cheese over the top. Add equal portions of the yellow beets and press down gently. Lift the cookie cutter up carefully to remove.

Drizzle each plate with 1 teaspoon of the dressing and sprinkle with the pistachios.

Mix the frisée and spinach in a bowl. Add the remaining dressing and toss to coat. Spoon equal portions of the salad carefully over each beet stack. Serve immediately.

ROSEMARY AND SAGE WHITE BEAN SPREAD

1¹/2 cups drained cooked white kidney beans
 (or other white bean)
2 tablespoons fresh lemon juice
3 tablespoons extra-virgin olive oil
2 teaspoons minced fresh rosemary
2 teaspoons minced fresh sage
¹/2 teaspoon kosher salt
¹/4 teaspoon freshly ground pepper
2 garlic cloves, minced
Sprig of rosemary or sage for garnish

Serves 6 to 8

*P*rocess the beans, lemon juice, olive oil, minced rosemary, minced sage, salt, pepper and garlic in a food processor until smooth. Remove to a serving bowl and garnish with a sprig of rosemary. Serve with baguette slices.

AUTUMN ROASTED CHICKEN

1 (4- to 5-pound) chicken
1 teaspoon freshly ground pepper
1 tablespoon kosher salt
¹/2 small onion
1 rib celery, cut into halves
4 teaspoons minced fresh thyme
4 teaspoons minced fresh rosemary

Serves 4 to 6

*R*inse the chicken and pat dry inside and out with paper towels. Sprinkle the pepper and some of the salt inside the cavity. Place the onion and celery in the cavity. Tie the legs together with kitchen twine and tuck the wings under the bird. Sprinkle the remaining salt evenly over the chicken. Sprinkle with the thyme and rosemary and place in a roasting pan.

Roast in a preheated 450-degree oven for 1¹/4 hours or to 165 degrees on a meat thermometer. Remove to a wire rack and let stand for 10 to 15 minutes before carving.

Harvest Stuffed Sugar Pumpkin

2 cups water or chicken stock
1 cup brown rice
2 teaspoons chicken base or chicken bouillon
    granules, or 1/4 teaspoon salt
3/4 to 1 teaspoon curry powder
1 pound bulk Italian turkey sausage or turkey
    breakfast sausage (hot or mild)
1/2 cup chopped onion
4 cups fresh mushrooms, sliced
1 large garlic clove, pressed
2 large shallots, minced (optional)
1/4 cup dry sherry
5 tablespoons currants
2 teaspoons salt
1 teaspoon garlic powder
1 teaspoon poultry seasoning
1/2 teaspoon sage
1/4 teaspoon marjoram
1 (4- to 5-pound) sugar pumpkin

Serves 6

Variation: Four to six small sugar pumpkins may be substituted for 1 large sugar pumpkin to make individual servings. Look for pumpkins with stems so that they can be baked and served with their tops for a more festive presentation.

*B*ring the water, rice, chicken base and curry powder to a boil in a 4-quart saucepan. Reduce the heat to low and stir. Simmer, covered, for 50 minutes. Remove from the heat and let stand, covered, for 10 to 15 minutes. Remove the lid and fluff the rice. Cover the pan and set aside.

Brown the sausage in a skillet, stirring until crumbly. Remove the sausage to paper towels to drain. Wipe out the skillet with a paper towel. Combine the onion, mushrooms, garlic and shallots in the skillet and sauté until tender. Reduce the heat to medium-low and stir in the sherry, sausage, currants, salt, garlic powder, poultry seasoning, sage and marjoram. Cook until the liquid is reduced, stirring frequently. Remove from the heat and stir in the rice.

Cut off the top of the pumpkin and remove the seeds and strings from the top and cavity. Spoon the rice mixture into the pumpkin cavity and replace the top. Place the pumpkin in a baking dish and add hot water to the baking dish to a depth of 1/2 inch. Bake in a preheated 350-degree oven for 1 1/2 hours or until the pumpkin is tender, adding more water to the baking dish as needed during baking to prevent sticking and burning. Cover the pumpkin loosely with foil after 30 minutes of baking if needed to prevent overbrowning. Cut the pumpkin into wedges and serve.

SAVORY ROASTED ROOT VEGETABLES

1/3 cup olive oil
2 tablespoons maple syrup
1 large garlic clove, minced
8 small purple potatoes, cut into
    1-inch pieces
2 large Yukon Gold potatoes, peeled and
    cut into 1-inch pieces
2 carrots, peeled and sliced diagonally
2 parsnips, peeled and chopped
2 large sweet potatoes, peeled and cut into
    1-inch pieces
1 large rutabaga, peeled and cut into
    1-inch pieces
2 large onions, cut into quarters
1 teaspoon salt, or to taste
1 tablespoon pepper, or to taste
1/3 cup chopped green onions

Serves 6 to 8

*W*hisk the olive oil, maple syrup and garlic in a small bowl. Spread the purple potatoes, Yukon Gold potatoes, carrots, parsnips, sweet potatoes, rutabaga and onions on a rimmed baking sheet. Drizzle the olive oil mixture over the vegetables and sprinkle with the salt and pepper. Roast in a preheated 350-degree oven for 1 1/2 hours or until the vegetables are tender and golden brown, stirring occasionally. Remove to a serving platter and sprinkle with the green onions.

Note: This is a versatile dish that provides a new way to serve vegetables in an attractive way.

*S*hortly after the leaves have turned from luscious green to the many beautiful colors of fall, plan a short drive up the Southern Indiana Knobs to Joe Huber's Family Farm. Enjoy a hayride out to the pumpkin patch and pick a pumpkin to place on your front porch and another to use for Harvest Stuffed Sugar Pumpkin (page 146). Have fun seeing who can find the biggest pumpkin!

TOK-SEL LIMA BEANS

1 pound fresh or frozen Fordhook lima beans
12 ounces pumpkin seeds
2 tablespoons sesame oil
2 bunches green onions, chopped
1 bunch parsley, chopped
Salt to taste
Lemon juice to taste

Serves 6

*B*lanch the lima beans in a saucepan of boiling water for 1 minute, drain. Spread the pumpkin seeds in a shallow baking pan. Roast in a preheated 350-degree oven until toasted, stirring occasionally. Grind the pumpkin seeds in a food processor and set aside. Heat the sesame oil in a large skillet over medium heat. Add the lima beans when the oil starts to smoke and sauté until the lima beans are golden brown and roasted. Add the green onions, parsley, salt and ground pumpkin seeds and sauté for 1 minute. Stir in lemon juice and serve.

Note: You may use preroasted pumpkin seeds instead of roasting them yourself.

Chef: Chef Bruce Ucán, Mayan Café

MAPLE BOURBON CIDER

3 ounces Kentucky bourbon
2 teaspoons fresh lemon juice
1 tablespoon maple syrup
1/2 cup apple cider
Lemon slices for garnish

Serves 2

*F*ill a cocktail shaker with ice. Add the bourbon, lemon juice, maple syrup and apple cider. Shake vigorously. Strain into glasses. Garnish each with a lemon slice and serve.

WHITE CHOCOLATE BREAD PUDDING WITH TART CHERRIES AND CARAMEL SAUCE

2 cups heavy cream
4 cups milk
1 cup sugar
2 cups chopped white chocolate
6 eggs
10 egg yolks
2 teaspoons vanilla extract
1/4 cup (1/2 stick) butter
1 loaf French bread, cut into 1/2-inch-
　　thick slices
2 cups dried tart cherries
Caramel Sauce (page 141)
Vanilla ice cream (optional)

Serves 6 to 8

Variation: Chill the baked bread pudding until cold, then loosen the pudding from the side of the pan with a small sharp knife. Place a cutting board over the pan and invert the pudding onto the cutting board. Remove the baking parchment. Cut the pudding into squares and arrange on a buttered baking sheet. Bake in a preheated 350-degree oven for 12 minutes. Serve as directed above.

Cook the cream, milk and sugar in a saucepan until hot, stirring constantly. Remove from the heat. Stir in the white chocolate until melted. Whisk the eggs, egg yolks and vanilla in a large bowl. Whisk a small amount of the hot cream mixture into the eggs. Add in the remaining hot cream very slowly, whisking constantly.

Coat a 9×13-inch baking pan with the butter and line the bottom of the pan with baking parchment Arrange half the bread slices over the bottom of the baking pan. Pour half the cream mixture evenly over the bread and sprinkle with half the cherries. Let stand for 5 to 10 minutes.

Arrange the remaining bread slices over the top and pour the remaining cream mixture over the bread. Sprinkle with the remaining cherries. Press on the bread with the back of a wooden spoon to make certain the bread is completely submerged. Cover the pan with foil and chill for at least 4 hours.

Bake, covered, in a preheated 325-degree oven for 1 hour. Remove the foil and bake for 30 minutes longer or until golden brown and most of the liquid has evaporated. Remove to a wire rack to cool slightly. Serve warm topped with Caramel Sauce and vanilla ice cream.

Winter

Roseheights Historic Home

Winter

The historic home of Roseheights, built in 1901 near Louisville's Cherokee Park, has hosted some of the city's most stately visitors, including Eleanor Roosevelt, presidents John F. Kennedy and Jimmy Carter, and poet Carl Sandberg. Entertain guests with a grand tablescape like this in the warmth of your own home by placing magnolia garlands above the fireplace. Beautiful, snowy white roses and hydrangeas nestled in silver heirlooms bring the wonder of winter indoors for a sophisticated holiday dinner party.

WINTER MENUS

Winter Chapter Sponsored by

White Clay Consulting

WHITE CLAY

Holiday Cocktail Party

Serves 12

BOURBON-SPICED PECANS

BACON-WRAPPED DATES

MERRIEST CAPRESE CUPS

MISTLETOE CRANBERRY SALSA

BEEF TENDERLOIN ON HERBED BISCUITS WITH
GORGONZOLA BUTTER

CRAB CAKES WITH RÉMOULADE

FLOURLESS DARK CHOCOLATE MINIS

EGGNOG CHEESECAKE BARS

HOLLYDAYS SUGAR COOKIES

POINSETTIA MARTINIS

Holiday Cocktail Party Menu Sponsored by

BITTNERS

Mistletoe Cranberry Salsa

BOURBON-SPICED PECANS

1/4 cup (1/2 stick) butter
2 cups pecan halves
1/4 cup Kentucky bourbon
2 tablespoons light brown sugar
1 tablespoon chopped dried rosemary
2 teaspoons Worcestershire sauce
2 teaspoons paprika
1 teaspoon cayenne pepper
1 teaspoon salt
1 teaspoon chili powder
1/4 teaspoon black pepper
1/8 teaspoon nutmeg
1/8 teaspoon cinnamon

Serves 16

Melt the butter in a skillet over medium heat. Add the pecans and sauté for 5 minutes or until lightly toasted. Stir in the bourbon. Stir in the brown sugar, rosemary, Worcestershire sauce, paprika, cayenne pepper, salt, chili powder, black pepper, nutmeg and cinnamon. Cook until the pecans are coated, stirring constantly. Cook for 1 to 2 minutes, stirring constantly. Spread the pecans evenly on a baking sheet. Cool completely, stirring occasionally to break apart the pecans.

BACON-WRAPPED DATES

24 large Medjool dates, pitted
4 ounces Brie cheese, rind removed
24 Marcona almonds
12 slices bacon, cut into halves crosswise

Serves 12

Make a lengthwise slit in each date. Cut the cheese into 24 equal pieces. Insert one piece of cheese and one almond into each date. Wrap one piece of bacon around each date and secure with a wooden pick. Arrange the dates on a baking sheet. Bake in a preheated 375-degree oven for 15 minutes or until the bacon is cooked through, turning over the dates halfway through cooking. Remove the dates to paper towels to drain and remove the wooden picks. Arrange in a serving bowl.

MERRIEST CAPRESE CUPS

16 miniature phyllo shells
8 grape tomatoes, halved
1 tablespoon extra-virgin olive oil
1 tablespoon balsamic vinegar
Salt and pepper to taste
4 ounces fresh mozzarella cheese, cut into
    16 cubes
3 large basil leaves

Serves 8

*A*rrange the phyllo shells on a baking sheet. Bake in a preheated 325-degree oven for 5 minutes or until the edges are light brown. Remove to a wire rack to cool completely. Combine the tomatoes, olive oil, vinegar, salt and pepper in a bowl and mix well. Place one cheese cube in the bottom of each phyllo shell and top each with one tomato half. Snip the basil with scissors over the top so that each cup has a sliver of basil on top. Serve immediately.

Note: While this makes a beautiful festive dish during the holidays, it's also a great recipe for summer if you can take advantage of ripe tomatoes. Phyllo cups can usually be found at the grocery store in the frozen section near the pies and frozen prepared desserts.

MISTLETOE CRANBERRY SALSA

2 small Granny Smith apples, peeled
    and chopped
1 serrano chile, chopped
1 teaspoon grated orange zest
1 orange, peeled, seeded and chopped
1/4 bunch cilantro, chopped
3/4 cup chopped red onion
8 ounces frozen cranberries
1/2 cup sugar
12 large endive leaves
6 ounces cream cheese, softened

Serves 12

*M*ix the apples, chile, orange zest, orange, cilantro and onion in a bowl. Combine the cranberries and sugar in a food processor and pulse to chop the cranberries. Add to the apple mixture and mix well. Let stand for 1 hour. Chill until ready to serve. Spoon 1 tablespoon of cream cheese onto the end of each endive leaf and top with the salsa.

Note: This salsa can be served with tortilla chips instead of endive and cream cheese.

BEEF TENDERLOIN ON HERBED BISCUITS WITH GORGONZOLA BUTTER

BEEF

2 tablespoons butter, softened
3 tablespoons Dijon mustard
2 teaspoons kosher salt
1 teaspoon freshly ground pepper
1 (2-pound) trimmed beef tenderloin

Serves 10 to 12

Combine the butter, Dijon mustard, salt and pepper in a bowl and mix well. Spread over the tenderloin. Place in a roasting pan and insert an ovenproof meat thermometer into the thickest part of the meat. Roast in a preheated 450-degree oven for 35 minutes or to 140 degrees on the meat thermometer for rare. Let cool to warm before cutting into 1/2-inch slices. Split each herbed biscuit and place one slice of warm tenderloin on the bottom halves of the biscuits. Spread with the Gorgonzola butter and place the biscuit halves on top.

Note: The biscuits can be made ahead and frozen. Freeze the unbaked biscuits on a baking sheet. Remove to a sealable plastic bag and keep in the freezer until ready to use. Arrange the frozen biscuits on a baking parchment-covered baking sheet and thaw slightly. Bake an additional 2 to 3 minutes. You can also assemble the sandwiches 1 to 2 hours in advance of serving. Wrap the sandwiches in foil and keep warm in a 150-degree oven.

HERBED BISCUITS

2 1/2 cups all-purpose flour
1 tablespoon baking powder
3/8 teaspoon salt
1/4 teaspoon baking soda
6 tablespoons cold unsalted butter, cut into
    small pieces
1 1/2 tablespoons finely chopped fresh thyme
1 1/2 tablespoons finely chopped fresh sage
1 1/4 cups buttermilk

Makes 20 to 24 biscuits

GORGONZOLA BUTTER

1/4 cup (1/2 stick) unsalted butter, softened
4 ounces Gorgonzola cheese, softened

Makes 3/4 cup

Whisk the flour, baking powder, salt and baking soda in a bowl. Cut in the cold butter with a pastry blender until crumbly. Add the thyme, sage and buttermilk and toss with a fork to form a sticky dough. Pat the dough out with floured hands on a floured work surface to 3/4 inch thick. Cut the dough with a 2-inch biscuit cutter to make 20 to 24 biscuits. Arrange the biscuits on a baking parchment-covered baking sheet. Bake in a preheated 450-degree oven for 17 minutes or until golden brown. Remove to a wire rack to cool.

Mix the butter and cheese in a bowl until smooth. Shape the mixture into a 4-inch log on a sheet of plastic wrap. Seal the plastic wrap around the log and chill for at least 1 hour or until firm. This can be made up to 1 week ahead and kept chilled.

The holidays are a busy time for everyone. Try throwing your next holiday party with a "bring your favorite cocktail recipe" theme. Ask guests to bring samples of their cocktail for everyone and copies of the recipe for those who can't get enough. This takes pressure off the host and allows guests to get new ideas for holiday entertaining in their own homes.

CRAB CAKES WITH RÉMOULADE

CRAB CAKES
3/4 cup mayonnaise
2 tablespoons minced garlic
1 tablespoon Sriracha sauce
2 tablespoons Tabasco sauce
2 tablespoons Creole mustard
1 teaspoon salt
1 teaspoon pepper
5 (6-ounce) cans lump crab meat, drained
Juice of 1/2 lemon
1 scallion, chopped
1/2 cup chopped red bell pepper
1/2 cup chopped red onion
1 1/2 cups (or more) panko bread crumbs
Vegetable oil

Makes 18 to 24 crab cakes

RÉMOULADE
1 pickle, chopped
2 tablespoons chopped red onion
1 teaspoon capers
1 cup mayonnaise
2 tablespoons Creole mustard
1 teaspoon chopped scallions
1 teaspoon chopped tarragon
1/2 teaspoon hot red pepper sauce
1/2 teaspoon Worcestershire sauce
1/2 teaspoon chili powder
Juice of 1/2 lemon
Salt and pepper to taste

Makes 1 1/4 cups

Whisk the mayonnaise, garlic, Sriracha sauce, Tabasco sauce, Creole mustard, salt and pepper in a bowl. Add the crab meat, lemon juice, scallion, bell pepper and onion and mix well, adding some of the bread crumbs if the mixture is too moist to form into patties. Chill for 30 minutes. Shape into 1 1/2-ounce patties. Spread the bread crumbs into a shallow dish and coat the patties in the bread crumbs. Heat oil in a skillet over medium heat. Add the crab cakes and fry for 4 to 5 minutes per side or until golden brown. Remove to paper towels to drain. Serve warm with rémoulade.

Combine the pickle, onion and capers in a food processor and pulse until finely chopped. Remove to a bowl. Add the mayonnaise, Creole mustard, scallions, tarragon, hot sauce, Worcestershire sauce, chili powder, lemon juice, salt and pepper and mix well.

Chef: Chef Michael Ton, Doc Crow's Southern Smokehouse & Raw Bar

FLOURLESS DARK CHOCOLATE MINIS

2 cups finely chopped or grated
   70% dark chocolate
1 3/4 cups (3 1/2 sticks) butter
8 egg yolks, at room temperature
1/2 cup granulated sugar
1 teaspoon brewed dark roast coffee or
   espresso (optional)
8 egg whites, at room temperature
Pinch of salt
1/2 cup granulated sugar
Confectioners' sugar
Whipped cream
Cinnamon or baking cocoa for garnish

Serves 12

Melt the chocolate and butter in the top of a double boiler over simmering water. Remove the top of the double boiler and let the chocolate mixture cool. Beat the egg yolks and 1/2 cup sugar in a mixing bowl until pale yellow. Stir in the cooled chocolate mixture. Stir in the coffee. Beat the egg whites and salt in a mixing bowl until frothy. Add 1/2 cup sugar and beat until soft peaks form. Fold the egg whites into the chocolate mixture.

Spoon into nonstick miniature muffin cups. Bake in a preheated 375-degree oven for 20 minutes or until a wooden pick inserted in the center comes out almost clean. Remove to a wire rack to cool completely. Remove the minis to decorative miniature muffin liners dusted with confectioners' sugar. Top with a dollop of whipped cream and garnish with cinnamon or baking cocoa.

Variation: This can be baked in a springform pan for 30 to 35 minutes instead of using miniature muffin cups.

The Hollydays Art and Gift Market, hosted by the Junior League of Louisville, is an annual event that is held the first weekend of December. The three-day shopping event includes scores of local vendors, children's events, and a silent auction. Funds raised at the event are returned to the community through projects focusing on improving the lives of women and children.

EGGNOG CHEESECAKE BARS

CRUST

1 cup all-purpose flour
1 cup packed brown sugar
3/4 teaspoon salt
1/2 cup (1 stick) cold butter, cut into pieces
1 cup pecan halves
3/4 cup rolled oats

Combine the flour, brown sugar, salt and butter in a food processor. Pulse until crumbly. Add the pecans and pulse until the pecans are chopped. Add the oats and process until the mixture is moistened but not clumping. Press over the bottom of a buttered and baking parchment-lined 9×13-inch baking pan. Bake in a preheated 350-degree oven for 15 minutes or until golden brown. Remove to a wire rack and pierce the crust ten times with a fork.

FILLING

12 ounces cream cheese, softened
3/4 cup sour cream
Seeds scraped from 2 vanilla beans
3 eggs
1/2 cup sugar
3 tablespoons all-purpose flour
1/4 teaspoon salt
1 cup eggnog

Serves 24

Beat the cream cheese, sour cream and vanilla seeds in a mixing bowl at medium speed until smooth. Add the eggs one at a time, beating well after each addition. Whisk the sugar, flour and salt in a bowl. Add to the cream cheese mixture and beat well. Beat in the eggnog at low speed just until combined. Pour over the baked crust. Bake in a preheated 325-degree oven for 40 minutes or until the center is almost set. Remove to a wire rack to cool completely. Chill overnight. Cut into bars and serve with Bourbon Cream on the side.

BOURBON CREAM

1 cup heavy whipping cream, chilled
3 tablespoons confectioners' sugar
2 tablespoons eggnog
2 teaspoons Kentucky bourbon
1/8 teaspoon nutmeg

Makes 2 cups

Combine the cream, confectioners' sugar, eggnog, bourbon and nutmeg in a chilled mixing bowl. Beat with chilled beaters at high speed until soft peaks form. Chill until ready to serve.

HOLLYDAYS SUGAR COOKIES

3 cups all-purpose flour
1 teaspoon baking powder
1 cup (2 sticks) unsalted butter, softened
1 cup granulated sugar
1 egg
1/2 teaspoon kosher salt
1 teaspoon vanilla extract
Dash of almond extract
2 1/2 cups confectioners' sugar
1 1/2 teaspoons butter, softened
1/4 cup milk
2 or 3 drops vanilla extract or almond extract
1 or 2 drops food coloring (optional)

Makes 4 dozen cookies

Note: If pure white frosting is desired, use clear vanilla extract and white butter in the frosting. Consider boxing 4 to 6 cookies for guests to take home as a party favor. Place the cookies in a small box, separated with waxed paper. Tie a ribbon around the box and include a personal message for a treat your guests will never forget.

*M*ix the flour and baking powder together. Beat 1 cup butter and the granulated sugar in a mixing bowl until light and fluffy. Beat in the egg, salt, 1 teaspoon vanilla and dash of almond extract. Stir in the dry ingredients 1 cup at a time. Shape the dough into a disc and wrap in plastic wrap. Chill for at least 1 hour.

Roll out the dough on a lightly floured surface to 1/2 inch thick. Cut with cookie cutters; arrange the cookies on a baking parchment-covered baking sheet. Bake in a preheated 375-degree oven for 8 to 10 minutes or until the edges of the cookies are golden brown. Cool on the cookie sheet for 5 minutes. Remove to a wire rack to cool completely. Beat the confectioners' sugar and 1 1/2 teaspoons butter in a mixing bowl. Beat in the milk, 2 drops of vanilla extract and the food coloring. Thin with a few drops of milk if the frosting is too thick. Frost the cooled cookies.

POINSETTIA MARTINIS

2 cups vodka
1 cup orange liqueur
1 cup pomegranate juice
1/2 cup freshly squeezed lime juice
8 strips of lime zest

Serves 8

*C*ombine the vodka, liqueur, pomegranate juice and lime juice in a pitcher. Chill until serving time. Pour the mixture into frozen martini glasses. Garnish each with a twist of lime zest and serve immediately.

New Year's Day

Serves 6 to 8

New Year's Fruit Salad

Hoppin' John Chowder

Goodluck Cabbage and Bow Tie Pasta

deSha's Corn Bread

Grapefruit and Pecan Cake

Bloody Marys

New Year's Day Menu Sponsored by
Jamie Estes, Estes Public Relations

ESTES
PUBLIC
RELATIONS

New Year's Fruit Salad

NEW YEAR'S FRUIT SALAD

2 cups water
1/2 cup sugar
1 (1-inch) piece fresh ginger, peeled and sliced
1 vanilla bean, split
1 lime
5 blood oranges
2 pears, peeled and chopped
1 pineapple, chopped
5 kiwifruit, chopped
12 kumquats, thinly sliced crosswise and
    seeds removed
1 cup pomegranate seeds

Serves 6

Combine the water, sugar and ginger in a saucepan. Scrape the seeds from the vanilla bean into the saucepan and add the bean. Peel wide strips of zest from the lime into the saucepan. Peel wide strips of zest from one of the oranges into the saucepan. Bring to a boil over medium-high heat, stirring frequently. Reduce the heat and simmer for 5 minutes. Remove from the heat and cool. Chill until cold. Peel all 5 oranges and section. Combine the orange sections, pears, pineapple, kiwifruit, kumquats and pomegranate seeds in a bowl and toss gently to mix. Add the chilled syrup and stir gently to mix. Chill overnight. Remove the citrus zest, ginger and vanilla bean before serving.

HOPPIN' JOHN CHOWDER

1 pound bulk sausage
1 (16-ounce) can tomatoes, chopped
3 (15-ounce) cans black-eyed peas
1 cup chopped onion
1 cup chopped celery
1 tablespoon salt
2 teaspoons (or more) chili powder
1/4 teaspoon dried basil leaves
1 bay leaf
1 cup cooked rice

Serves 6

Brown the sausage in a large saucepan, stirring until crumbly; drain. Stir in the tomatoes and peas. Add the onion, celery, salt, chili powder, basil and bay leaf and stir to mix. Simmer, covered, for 1 to 1 1/2 hours. Stir in the rice. Simmer, covered, for 20 minutes. Remove the bay leaf and serve.

GOOD LUCK CABBAGE AND BOW TIE PASTA

1/4 cup olive oil
3 or 4 garlic cloves, chopped
1/4 cup chopped onion
1/2 cup chopped country ham or corned beef
1/2 head cabbage, shredded
1/4 teaspoon crushed red pepper flakes
Salt and pepper to taste
8 ounces bow tie pasta, cooked and drained
1/2 cup (2 ounces) grated Parmesan cheese

Serves 4 to 6

*H*eat the olive oil in a nonstick skillet. Add the garlic, onion and ham and sauté until the garlic and onion are golden brown. Remove to a bowl. Add the cabbage, red pepper flakes, salt and pepper to the skillet and reduce the heat to low. Cook, covered, for 20 minutes or until the cabbage is tender, stirring every 5 minutes. Stir in the ham mixture and pasta and toss to mix. Cook until heated through. Remove to a serving bowl and sprinkle with the cheese.

Variation: You may use cauliflower instead of cabbage.

*E*ating "good luck" foods on New Year's Day is a tradition that is practiced all over the world. Cooked greens such as cabbage and kale resemble money and are thought to be symbols of good fortune. Legumes, pork, and corn bread are also thought to bring good luck. But there are some foods that the superstitious would advise staying away from: lobsters move backward, and eating the crustacean on New Year's Day symbolizes setbacks.

167

deSha's Corn Bread

3 cups self-rising cornmeal
1/3 cup sugar
6 eggs
3/4 cup vegetable oil
3 cups sour cream
2 2/3 cup cream-style corn
1 1/4 cups (2 1/2 sticks) butter, softened
1/2 cup honey

Serves 15

Combine the cornmeal, sugar, eggs, oil, sour cream and corn in a bowl and mix well. Pour into a nonstick 9×13-inch baking pan. Bake in a preheated 350-degree oven for 30 minutes. Remove to a wire rack to cool. Combine the butter and honey in a bowl and mix well. Serve the corn bread with the honey butter on the side.

Note: Recipe compliments of deSha's.

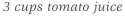

Bloody Marys

3 cups tomato juice
3 tablespoons lemon juice
3 tablespoons lime juice
1 tablespoon prepared horseradish
1 tablespoon Worcestershire sauce
1 teaspoon minced garlic
2 teaspoons hot sauce
1 3/4 tablespoons celery salt
3/4 teaspoon ground pepper
4 ounces vodka

Serves 4

Combine the tomato juice, lemon juice, lime juice, horseradish, Worcestershire sauce, garlic, hot sauce, celery salt and pepper in a blender and purée until smooth. Fill four glasses with ice. Add 1 ounce vodka to each glass. Fill with the Bloody Mary mix. Best when served very cold.

Note: Garnish with pepperoncinis, cocktail onions, stuffed olives, celery sticks, dill pickled beans, or pickles.

Create a New Year's resolution to buy local and get off to a great start. Weisenberger Flour Mill makes self-rising cornmeal that's ground from locally grown yellow corn and works perfectly in deSha's Corn Bread. This family-owned and operated mill has been "the baker's choice" since 1865. Visit the mill, buy online, or purchase from select specialty food shops.

GRAPEFRUIT AND PECAN CAKE

CAKE

1 cup (2 sticks) unsalted butter
1/2 cup fresh grapefruit juice
1/2 cup water
2 cups all-purpose flour, sifted
1 cup granulated sugar
1 cup packed brown sugar
1 teaspoon baking soda
1/2 teaspoon cinnamon
1/4 teaspoon kosher salt
2 tablespoons grated grapefruit zest
1 cup toasted pecans, coarsely chopped
1/2 cup buttermilk
2 eggs, lightly beaten
2 teaspoons vanilla extract
1/2 cup toasted pecans, coarsely chopped

Serves 16

GRAPEFRUIT FROSTING

8 ounces cream cheese, softened
1/2 cup (1 stick) unsalted butter, softened
2 teaspoons grated grapefruit zest
1 teaspoon vanilla extract
4 cups confectioners' sugar

Makes 2 1/2 cups

Combine the butter, grapefruit juice and water in a saucepan. Cook over low heat until the butter is melted, stirring occasionally; set aside. Mix the flour, granulated sugar, brown sugar, baking soda, cinnamon and salt in a large bowl. Stir in the grapefruit zest and 1 cup pecans. Add the butter mixture, buttermilk, eggs and vanilla and mix well. Pour into a greased and floured 9×13-inch baking pan. Bake in a preheated 375-degree oven for 20 to 30 minutes or until a wooden pick inserted in the center comes out clean. Remove to a wire rack to cool. Spread the grapefruit frosting over the cooled cake and sprinkle with 1/2 cup pecans.

Beat the cream cheese, butter, grapefruit zest and vanilla in a bowl until creamy. Beat in the confectioners' sugar gradually until light and fluffy.

Soup Night

Serves 6 to 8

CRISPY KALE

CRUNCHY WINTER SALAD

BEEF AND BEAN CHILI WITH GUACAMOLE

ROASTED CORN CHOWDER WITH CHICKEN AND CILANTRO

LENTIL SOUP

SAGE SAUSAGE MINESTRONE

FIRESIDE ONION TART

CHEESE PUFFS

PUMPKIN BROWNIE WITH ICE CREAM AND CARAMEL

SPICED CRANBERRY SIPPER

Soup Night Menu Sponsored by

Foxhollow Farm

FOXHOLLOW
FARM

Crispy Kale

CRISPY KALE

1 bunch kale, stems removed
2 tablespoons olive oil
Pinch of salt
Pinch of pepper

Serves 4

*C*hop the kale into pieces the size of potato chips and spread on a baking sheet. Drizzle with the olive oil and sprinkle with the salt and pepper. Toss the kale and spread into a single layer. Bake on the middle rack in a preheated 400-degree oven for 8 to 10 minutes or until crisp. Remove to a wire rack to cool.

CRUNCHY WINTER SALAD

1 bunch red leaf lettuce, chopped
1 cup walnuts, toasted
1 Red Delicious apple, finely chopped
1 Granny Smith apple, finely chopped
3/4 cup crumbled blue cheese
1/2 cup dried cranberries
1 tablespoon Dijon mustard
1 tablespoon honey
2 tablespoons red wine vinegar
6 tablespoons extra-virgin olive oil
Dash of pepper

Serves 6

*C*ombine the lettuce, walnuts, apples, cheese and cranberries in a bowl and toss to mix. Whisk the Dijon mustard, honey, vinegar, olive oil and pepper in a bowl. Drizzle over the salad and toss to coat. Serve immediately.

*H*ead to Foxhollow Farm in Crestwood, Kentucky, and stop into The Farm Store to gather many of the ingredients used in this menu. Grab some grass-fed beef to use in Beef and Bean Chili (page 173) and all the veggies you need to round out this hearty meal. Foxhollow is a growing group of individuals and families committed to building a sustainable and biodynamic farm community. Food from Foxhollow can also be found at the St. Matthew's Farmers' Market and many local restaurants.

BEEF AND BEAN CHILI WITH GUACAMOLE

CHILI

1 (15-ounce) can black beans, drained
   and rinsed
1 (14-ounce) can diced tomatoes
1 canned chipotle chile plus 2 tablespoons
   of the adobo sauce
2 tablespoons extra-virgin olive oil
1 pound lean ground beef
1/2 teaspoon kosher salt
1 garlic clove, minced
1/2 large red onion, finely chopped
1/4 teaspoon kosher salt
1 1/2 tablespoons chili powder
2 teaspoons ground cumin
Pinch of cayenne pepper, or to taste
2 (15-ounce) cans pinto beans, drained
   and rinsed
Juice of 1/2 lime
1/4 cup chopped fresh cilantro
Kosher salt to taste
Freshly ground black pepper to taste
1/4 cup chopped fresh cilantro

Serves 4

GUACAMOLE

1 avocado, chopped
Juice of 1/2 lime
1/2 large red onion, finely chopped
Kosher salt and pepper to taste

Serves 4

Process the black beans, tomatoes, chipotle chili and adobo sauce in a food processor until smooth. Heat the olive oil in a 5- to 6-quart heavy saucepan over medium-high heat for 2 minutes or until shimmering. Add the ground beef and 1/2 teaspoon salt and cook, stirring until crumbly. Remove the ground beef with a slotted spoon to paper towels to drain.

Add the garlic, onion and 1/4 teaspoon salt to the saucepan and sauté for 3 minutes or until the onion is tender. Reduce the heat to medium. Stir in the chili powder, cumin and cayenne pepper and cook for 20 seconds, stirring constantly. Stir in the pinto beans, black bean mixture and ground beef.

Simmer for 10 minutes, stirring frequently. Stir in the lime juice and 1/4 cup cilantro and season with salt and black pepper to taste. Thin the chili with a small amount of water if it seems too thick. Ladle into serving bowls. Top with the guacamole and sprinkle with 1/4 cup cilantro.

Combine the avocado, lime juice, onion, salt and pepper in a bowl and mix gently.

173

ROASTED CORN CHOWDER WITH CHICKEN AND CILANTRO

1 tablespoon extra-virgin olive oil
1 teaspoon ground cumin
1/2 teaspoon curry powder, chili powder or
   chili paste, or to taste
4 or 5 garlic cloves, chopped
1 sweet onion, chopped
3 ears corn, roasted and kernels cut
   from the cob
1 large sweet potato, peeled and chopped
1 (14-ounce) can fire-roasted diced tomatoes
   with green chiles
1 cup chopped seeded fresh heirloom tomatoes
4 ounces roasted green chiles, chopped
1 quart (4 cups) vegetable broth
1 (14-ounce) can coconut milk or plain
   hemp milk
2 cups shredded cooked chicken
Sea salt and freshly ground pepper to taste
Organic raw agave to taste
3 tablespoons chopped fresh cilantro
Juice of 2 limes
Lime wedges for garnish
Shredded Mexican cheese for garnish

Serves 8

*H*eat the olive oil in a large saucepan over medium heat. Add the cumin and curry powder and cook for 1 minute, stirring constantly. Add the garlic and onion and sauté for 5 minutes. Add the corn, sweet potatoes, fire-roasted tomatoes, fresh tomatoes and green chiles and sauté for 1 minute. Stir in the broth. Cook, covered, to almost boiling. Reduce the heat and simmer, covered, for 20 minutes or until the potatoes are tender.

Stir in the coconut milk and chicken. Season with salt and pepper and drizzle with agave. Cook gently until heated through; do not let boil. Stir in the cilantro and lime juice. Ladle into serving bowls and garnish each serving with a lime wedge and cheese.

Note: The lime juice brightens the taste and accents the spice. The agave cools the hotness.

If fresh corn is not in season, you may roast thawed frozen corn kernels.

This chowder works well made in a slow-cooker. Add the coconut milk and chicken 30 minutes before serving and add the lime juice and cilantro just before serving.

LENTIL SOUP

1/4 cup olive oil
1 large onion, chopped
1 pound lentils, rinsed and drained
3 ribs celery, chopped
1 (12-ounce) package baby carrots, chopped,
    or 3 large carrots, chopped
1 (14-ounce) can petite-diced tomatoes
2 tablespoons oregano
6 cups water, beef broth or chicken broth
Vinegar (optional)

Serves 6 to 8

*H*eat the olive oil in a large saucepan. Add the onion and sauté until translucent. Stir in the lentils, celery, carrots, tomatoes, oregano and water. Bring to a boil. Reduce the heat and simmer for 45 to 60 minutes or until the lentils are tender. Ladle into serving bowls and add 1 tablespoon vinegar to each serving.

Note: This recipe was provided by the First Lady of Louisville, Dr. Alexandra Gerassimides.

SAGE SAUSAGE MINESTRONE

1 pound bulk sage sausage
2 tablespoons olive oil
1 large onion, chopped
4 garlic cloves, minced
2 ribs celery, chopped
1 large carrot, chopped
1 teaspoon each dried basil, oregano and thyme
3/4 teaspoon kosher salt
Freshly ground pepper to taste
1 (28-ounce) can diced tomatoes
1 (15-ounce) can crushed tomatoes
6 cups chicken broth
1 (15-ounce) can kidney beans
1 cup chopped collard greens
1 cup macaroni, cooked and drained
Pinch of kosher salt
1/3 cup grated Parmesan cheese
2 tablespoons chopped fresh basil

Serves 8

*B*rown the sausage in a large saucepan, stirring until crumbly; drain. Remove the sausage to paper towels to drain. Heat the olive oil in a stockpot over medium-high heat. Add the onion and sauté for 4 minutes or until translucent. Add the garlic and sauté for 30 seconds. Add the celery and carrot and sauté for 5 minutes or until softened. Add the dried basil, oregano, thyme, 3/4 teaspoon salt and pepper and cook for 3 minutes, stirring constantly. Stir in the tomatoes, sausage and broth. Bring to a boil. Reduce the heat to medium-low and simmer for 10 minutes.

Drain and rinse the kidney beans. Stir the beans and collard greens into the soup. Cook for 10 minutes or until the greens are tender. Stir in the macaroni and pinch of salt. Ladle into serving bowls and top with the cheese and fresh basil.

FIRESIDE ONION TART

1 tablespoon olive oil
2 1/2 pounds yellow onions, sliced
2 large shallots, sliced
2 tablespoons chopped fresh thyme
3/4 teaspoon kosher salt
1/4 teaspoon pepper
1 refrigerated pie pastry
1/4 cup crumbed feta cheese
1/3 cup shredded Gruyère cheese
1 egg, lightly beaten
2 tablespoons water

Serves 6

Heat the olive oil in a large skillet over medium-high heat. Add the onions, shallots, thyme, salt and pepper and cook for 20 minutes, stirring occasionally. Unroll the pastry on a baking parchment-covered baking sheet. Sprinkle the feta cheese over the pastry, leaving a 1 1/2-inch border around the edge. Spread the onion mixture evenly over the feta cheese and sprinkle with the Gruyère cheese.

Fold in the edge of the pastry and pleat to form a rim. Mix the egg and water in a small bowl and brush over the pastry edge. Bake in a preheated 425-degree oven for 25 minutes or until the bottom of the crust is golden brown. Cool for 10 minutes before serving.

Variation: You may use reduced-fat feta cheese and can also substitute Swiss cheese for the Gruyère cheese.

Kentuckians get to enjoy all four seasons and it's a known fact they do not escape "Old Man Winter." With an average of eighty to ninety days with temperatures below freezing, use this menu as an excuse to invite some friends over to warm up over soup. Throw down a blanket in front of the fireplace for a cozy winter picnic.

CHEESE PUFFS

1/2 cup milk
6 tablespoons unsalted butter
1/4 cup water
1/2 teaspoon sea salt
Dash of white pepper
Dash of ground red pepper
3/4 cup all-purpose flour
1/4 teaspoon baking powder
3 eggs
3/4 cup (3 ounces) shredded Gruyère cheese
1 tablespoon milk

Serves 12

Combine 1/2 cup milk, the butter, water, salt, white pepper and cayenne pepper in a heavy saucepan. Cook over medium heat until the butter is melted, stirring occasionally. Add the flour and baking powder and stir briskly until the dough pulls away from the side of the pan. Reduce the heat to low and cook for 2 minutes, stirring constantly. Remove from the heat and let cool for 5 minutes. Add the eggs one at a time, beating well after each addition. Reserve 2 tablespoons of the cheese and stir the remaining cheese into the dough.

Drop the dough by level tablespoonfuls onto a baking parchment-covered baking sheet. Brush the tops with 1 tablespoon milk and sprinkle with the reserved cheese. Bake in a preheated 400-degree oven for 18 to 20 minutes or until golden brown. Serve hot or warm.

Variation: Almost any flavorful cheese works in this recipe. Try Cheddar cheese and 3 slices crumbled cooked bacon, or use 1/4 cup crumbled blue cheese and 1/4 cup finely chopped pecans.

PUMPKIN BROWNIES WITH ICE CREAM AND CARAMEL

1 cup all-purpose flour
1 teaspoon baking powder
1/4 teaspoon salt
3/4 teaspoon cinnamon
1/4 teaspoon ginger
1/8 (heaping) teaspoon ground cloves
1/2 cup (1 stick) unsalted butter, softened
1 cup packed brown sugar
1 egg
1 teaspoon vanilla extract
3/4 cup canned pumpkin
1/2 cup coarsely chopped pecans
2 ounces cream cheese, softened
2 tablespoons granulated sugar
1 egg yolk
2 teaspoons whipping cream
1/2 teaspoon vanilla extract
Caramel Sauce (page 141)
Vanilla ice cream or frozen yogurt

Serves 8

*M*ix the flour, baking powder, salt, cinnamon, ginger and cloves together. Beat the butter in a mixing bowl until light and fluffy. Beat in the brown sugar gradually and beat for 2 minutes. Beat in the egg and 1 teaspoon vanilla. Beat in the dry ingredients until well combined. Beat in the pumpkin. Stir in the pecans.

Spread the batter in a buttered and floured 8×8-inch baking dish. Beat the cream cheese, granulated sugar, egg yolk, cream and 1/2 teaspoon vanilla in a bowl. Dollop the cream cheese mixture over the batter. Swirl through the batter gently with a knife to create a marbled effect. Bake in a preheated 350-degree oven for 35 to 40 minutes or until the top is firm and a wooden pick inserted in the center comes out clean.

Warm the Caramel Sauce in a saucepan over low heat. Cut the warm brownies into squares and place on serving plates. Top the brownies with a scoop of ice cream and drizzle with warm Caramel Sauce.

Note: You may purchase caramel sauce rather than making it. The brownies can be made one day ahead. Keep covered with foil at room temperature. Warm the brownies in a preheated 350-degree oven for 15 minutes before cutting and serving.

SPICED CRANBERRY SIPPER

64 ounces cran-raspberry or
    cran-pomegranate juice cocktail
1/2 cup packed brown sugar
2 cups semi-dry red wine
4 sticks cinnamon
1/2 teaspoon whole cloves

Serves 12

Combine the cran-raspberry juice and brown sugar in a large kettle or stockpot. Heat over medium-high heat until the sugar is dissolved, stirring frequently. Add the wine, cinnamon and cloves. Heat until nearly boiling; reduce heat and simmer for 15 minutes; do not boil. Remove from the heat and strain into mugs or heat-resistant cups, discarding the solids. Serve hot.

Note: You can substitute Southern Savannah Cinnamon Mix for the spices. It can be found at local specialty food shops.

Take a break from the traditional chili cook-off and invite your friends over for a competition that will be sure to heat up the kitchen on a cold winter night. Divide your guests into two or three teams, but be sure to reserve a few guests as judges. Provide your competitors with an array of ingredients and equipment that can be used to make an award-winning soup and let the games begin. If you want to make this even more of a challenge, go Iron Chef style and mandate a special ingredient (for example, Italian sausage, butternut squash, or kale). The winning team will have bragging rights until the competition heats up again.

Snow Day

Serves 4

BREAKFAST

BANANA PANCAKES

LUNCH

COZY, CREAMY TOMATO BASIL SOUP

SNOW ANGEL CHEESE PANINI

BACON JAM

SNACKS

PLEASIN' PIZZA POPCORN

FIRST LADY'S PEANUT BUTTER COOKIES

BABY IT'S COLD OUTSIDE HOT CHOCOLATE

Snow Day Menu Sponsored by

Algood Food Company

Cozy, Creamy Tomato Basil Soup

BANANA PANCAKES

2 cups all-purpose flour
1 tablespoon sugar
1 tablespoon baking powder
1/2 teaspoon salt
1 egg
1 3/4 cups milk
1 teaspoon vanilla extract
2 tablespoons vegetable oil or canola oil
2 very ripe bananas, mashed until smooth
Additional vegetable oil or canola oil
1 cup maple syrup
1 tablespoon Algood peanut butter

Serve 4 to 6

Variation: For a special treat, sprinkle peanut butter chips on the pancakes just before turning over. Your kids will "go bananas".

*W*hisk the flour, sugar, baking powder and salt in a large bowl. Whisk the egg, milk, vanilla and 2 tablespoons oil in a bowl. Add to the dry ingredients and stir until almost smooth. Add the bananas and stir until smooth.

Heat a griddle to 400 degrees or heat a skillet over medium to medium-high heat until a drop of water sizzles when added. Heat a small amount of oil on the griddle. Pour 1/4 cup of batter onto the griddle to make a 4-inch pancake. Turn the pancake over when the top is bubbly and the edges begin to brown. Cook until golden brown on the bottom. Remove to a serving platter and keep warm. Repeat with the remaining batter.

Mix the maple syrup and peanut butter in a microwave-safe bowl. Microwave on High for 20 to 30 seconds. Stir until blended. Serve the pancakes with the peanut butter maple syrup or top the pancakes with peanut butter and jelly.

182

*A*verage snowfall in Kentucky ranges from 10 inches in the west to 25 inches in the extreme northeast, so parents can plan on at least one snow day every school year. When the kids are snowed in, consider inviting the neighbors and their children over for hot chocolate and make-your-own marshmallows. Place marshmallows on toothpicks or skewers and dip in chocolate. Raid your pantry for tasty toppings such as crushed graham crackers or cookies, coconut, sprinkles, miniature chocolate chips, dried cranberries, crushed banana chips, or chopped nuts.

COZY, CREAMY TOMATO BASIL SOUP

2 tablespoons olive oil
2 shallots, chopped
2 (15-ounce) cans chicken broth
1 (28-ounce) can crushed tomatoes
2 tablespoons basil pesto
1 cup heavy cream
1 teaspoon each salt and pepper
12 basil leaves, chopped

Serves 4

*H*eat the olive oil in a saucepan. Add the shallots and sauté for 2 to 3 minutes or until tender. Stir in the broth and tomatoes. Bring to a boil over medium-high heat. Stir in the pesto, cream, salt and pepper and reduce the heat to low. Simmer for 15 minutes, stirring occasionally. Purée in batches in a blender. Pour into serving bowls and garnish with the basil.

SNOW ANGEL CHEESE PANINI

1/4 cup (1/2 stick) butter, softened
8 slices sourdough bread
3 ounces white Cheddar cheese, shredded
3 ounces Gruyère cheese, shredded
3 ounces provolone cheese, shredded
3 ounces mozzarella cheese, shredded

Serves 4

Variation: Have fun switching this recipe up. On the first big snow of the year, add Bacon Jam (page 184) to the sandwiches before grilling. Other variations to try: thinly sliced Granny Smith apple, thinly sliced tomato and fresh basil, or sliced pineapple and thinly sliced ham.

*S*pread the butter evenly on one side of each bread slice. Combine the Cheddar cheese, Gruyère cheese, provolone cheese and mozzarella cheese in a bowl and toss to mix. Spread equal portions of the cheese on the unbuttered side of 4 bread slices. Top with the remaining bread slices buttered side up.

Heat a large cast-iron skillet or griddle over medium-high heat. Arrange the sandwiches in the skillet and cover with foil. Place a smaller heavy skillet on the foil to "press" the sandwiches. Cook for 3 minutes per side or until golden brown and the cheese is melted. If you have a panini maker, cook the sandwiches for 7 to 8 minutes on medium heat.

BACON JAM

1¹/2 pounds bacon, cut into 1-inch pieces
Cayenne pepper to taste
2 sweet Vidalia onions, chopped
3 garlic cloves, crushed
¹/4 cup cider vinegar
¹/4 cup balsamic vinegar
¹/2 cup packed dark brown sugar
¹/4 cup pure maple syrup

Makes 2 cups

Note: Bacon jam is great over grits, on biscuits, sandwiches, hamburgers, bread, or crackers.

Season the bacon with cayenne pepper in a large skillet. Cook over medium-high heat for 20 minutes or until the bacon is light brown, stirring occasionally. Remove the bacon to paper towels to drain. Remove and discard all but 1 tablespoon of bacon drippings from the skillet.

Add the onions and garlic to the skillet and sauté for 6 minutes or until the onions are translucent. Stir in the cider vinegar, balsamic vinegar, brown sugar, maple syrup and a dash of cayenne pepper. Bring to a boil and cook for 2 minutes, scraping any browned bits from the bottom of the skillet and stirring constantly. Stir in the bacon. Remove the mixture to a 6-quart slow cooker. Cook, uncovered, on High for 3¹/2 to 4 hours or until the liquid is syrupy. Remove to a food processor and coarsely chop, if desired. Remove to a bowl and let cool before serving. Store any leftovers in a sealed container in the refrigerator for up to 4 weeks.

PLEASIN' PIZZA POPCORN

1 tablespoon olive oil or melted butter
8 cups popped popcorn
3 tablespoons grated Parmesan cheese
1 teaspoon garlic powder
1 teaspoon Italian seasoning
1 teaspoon paprika
¹/2 teaspoon salt
¹/4 teaspoon pepper

Makes 8 cups

Drizzle the olive oil over the popcorn in a large bowl and toss to coat. Whisk the cheese, garlic powder, Italian seasoning, paprika, salt and pepper in a bowl or combine in a jar with a tight-fitting lid and shake to mix. Sprinkle over the popcorn and toss to coat.

Note: End your day inside with a movie and this tasty popcorn.

FIRST LADY'S PEANUT BUTTER COOKIES

1 cup creamy Algood peanut butter
1/2 cup granulated sugar
1 cup packed brown sugar
2 eggs
1 teaspoon vanilla extract
2 teaspoons baking soda
1/2 teaspoon salt
1 cup raw sugar

Make 2 dozen

*B*eat the peanut butter, granulated sugar and brown sugar in a mixing bowl. Add the eggs and vanilla and mix well. Add the baking soda and salt and mix well. Shape the dough into small balls and coat in the raw sugar. Arrange the balls on a baking parchment-covered cookie sheet. Bake in a preheated 350-degree oven for 12 minutes. Cool on the cookie sheet for 2 minutes. Remove to a wire rack to cool completely. For a fun cookie for kids, add 1/2 teaspoon of jam on top of each cookie when removed from the oven.

Note: Recipe compliments of the First Lady of Kentucky, Jane Beshear.

BABY IT'S COLD OUTSIDE HOT CHOCOLATE

1 1/2 cups baking cocoa
1 1/4 cups sugar
1 cup miniature chocolate chips
1/4 teaspoon salt
Milk

Makes 3 1/2 cups mix

*M*ix the baking cocoa, sugar, chocolate chips and salt in a bowl. Store in an airtight container at room temperature for up to 6 months.

For each serving, combine 3 tablespoons cocoa mixture and 1 cup milk in a saucepan. Cook over medium-high heat until hot and the chocolate chips are melted, stirring constantly. Serve in mugs. Top with toasted marshmallows or add peppermint extract or caramel flavoring for a special treat.

*M*ake this hot chocolate extraordinary by using JD Country Milk. This family-owned and operated dairy farm and processing plant located in Logan County, Kentucky is dedicated to providing quality, hormone-free milk. JD Country Milk can be found at many local specialty food shops or on the farm, where you can also buy a variety of cheeses, farm eggs, and homemade sweet cream butter.

Valentine's Day Dinner

Serves 4

Luscious Fig Crostini

Perfect Pair Marinated Olives

Spicy Oyster Caesar Salad

Basil Love Letters with Brown Butter Sauce

Spicy Seabass with Forbidden Rice

Sweetheart Hazelnut Mousse

Ginger Champagne

Luscious Fig Crostini

LUSCIOUS FIG CROSTINI

1 baguette, sliced
Extra-virgin olive oil
4 ounces ricotta cheese
1/2 pint Black Mission figs, coarsely chopped
Honey
Freshly cracked pepper to taste
Fig leaves for garnish

Serves 4

*B*rush both sides of the bread slices with olive oil. Heat a grill pan over medium-high heat. Add the bread and toast until golden brown, about 2 to 3 minutes per side. Remove to a work surface. Spread the cheese lightly over each bread slice and top with the figs. Drizzle with honey and sprinkle with pepper. Arrange on a platter and garnish with fig leaves.

PERFECT PAIR MARINATED OLIVES

1 teaspoon each fennel seeds and cumin seeds
3/4 cup green Spanish olives
1/2 cup black Spanish olives
1 teaspoon each orange zest and lemon zest
1 shallot, finely chopped
Pinch of cinnamon
2 tablespoons red wine vinegar
3 tablespoons extra-virgin olive oil
1 tablespoon orange juice
1 teaspoon each chopped fresh mint and parsley

Serves 4

*R*oast the fennel seeds and cumin seeds in a dry skillet until they begin to pop, stirring frequently. Remove to a bowl. Add the green olives, black olives, orange zest, lemon zest, shallot and cinnamon and toss to mix. Whisk the vinegar, olive oil, orange juice, mint and parsley in a bowl. Drizzle over the olive mixture and toss well. Chill, covered, for several hours before serving.

Note: Serve with meats and cheeses.

*S*ave yourself time and money by planning a romantic evening at home with your loved one on Valentine's Day. We've helped you out by creating a menu that was intentionally planted with foods that arouse the senses. Honey, figs, olives, oysters, basil, sea bass, hazelnuts, and ginger are all aphrodisiacs. Science suggests that much of the aphrodisiac effect appears to be psychological, heightened by the senses of sight and smell in addition to taste. So sit down for a romantic meal and hope for a night to remember.

SPICY OYSTER CAESAR SALAD

SALAD
3/4 cup all-purpose flour
3 tablespoons cayenne pepper
2 tablespoons filé powder
6 tablespoons salt
1 1/2 tablespoons onion powder
1 1/2 tablespoons garlic powder
1 1/2 tablespoons white pepper
1 1/2 tablespoons black pepper
1 1/2 tablespoons paprika
20 oysters
Peanut oil
1 head romaine, chopped
2 slices bacon, crisp-cooked and crumbled
1 roasted red bell pepper, sliced or chopped
1/2 cup brioche croutons
Grated Parmesan cheese

Serves 4

CAESAR DRESSING
1/4 cup red wine vinegar
1 1/2 teaspoons anchovy paste
1 1/2 teaspoons chopped garlic
1 tablespoon Worcestershire sauce
1/2 cup (2 ounces) grated Parmesan cheese
Dash of Tabasco sauce
1 cup olive oil

Makes 1 3/4 cups

*W*hisk the flour, cayenne pepper, filé powder, salt, onion powder, garlic powder, white pepper, black pepper and paprika in a bowl. Dredge the oysters one at a time in the flour mixture to generously coat. Pour peanut oil into a frying pan to a depth of 1 inch and heat until hot. Add the oysters and fry for 2 minutes or until crispy. Remove to paper towels to drain and keep warm. Combine the romaine and 1/4 cup of the Caesar dressing in a bowl and toss to coat. Divide among four salad plates. Top each with equal portions of the bacon, roasted pepper and croutons. Top each salad with five oysters and sprinkle with cheese.

Note: For less heat, use additional flour.

*P*rocess the vinegar, anchovy paste, garlic, Worcestershire sauce, cheese and Tabasco sauce in a blender or food processor until smooth. Add the olive oil in a fine stream, processing constantly until smooth.

Chef: Chef Shawn Ward, Jack Fry's

BASIL LOVE LETTERS WITH BROWN BUTTER SAUCE

1/4 cup (1/2 stick) butter
2 shallots, chopped
2 garlic cloves, chopped
Kosher salt to taste
1 pound green peas, fresh or frozen
2 cups fresh basil leaves
1 cup (4 ounces) grated Parmesan cheese
1/2 cup heavy cream
Freshly ground pepper to taste
Grated zest of 1 lemon
16 (3-inch) fresh pasta wrappers or
    won ton wrappers
1/2 cup (1 stick) unsalted butter,
    cut into 8 slices
1/4 cup pine nuts, toasted

Serves 4

Melt 1/4 cup butter in a heavy saucepan. Add the shallots and garlic and sauté until tender. Remove from the heat and let cool. Bring 3 quarts of lightly salted water in a saucepan to a boil. Add the peas and cook for 1 to 2 minutes or until tender but still bright green. Remove with a slotted spoon to a bowl of ice water for 1 minute to stop the cooking process. Remove the peas with a slotted spoon to paper towels to drain.

Set aside sixteen of the basil leaves for garnish. Add the remaining basil to the boiling water and blanch for a few seconds. Drain and remove the basil leaves to the ice water for 1 minute to stop the cooking process; drain. Spread the basil leaves over paper towels and dry well.

Combine the peas, basil, cheese, cream, shallot mixture, salt and pepper in a food processor and pulse until smooth. Add the lemon zest and pulse to mix. Lay the pasta wrappers on a work surface. Spoon 1 teaspoon of the pea mixture onto the center of each pasta wrapper and fold over the filling to form a rectangle. Press the edges to seal.

Bring 6 quarts of lightly salted water in a saucepan to a boil. Add the ravioli and cook for 2 to 3 minutes or until tender; drain. Divide the ravioli among four serving plates.

Heat a thick-bottomed skillet over medium heat. Add 1/2 cup unsalted butter and cook until light brown specks appear and the butter has a nutty aroma, whisking constantly and watching so that the butter doesn't burn. Remove from the heat and place on a cool heatproof surface to stop the cooking process.

Top the ravioli with the butter sauce and sprinkle with the pine nuts. Garnish with the reserved basil leaves.

Note: The uncooked ravioli can be refrigerated for a few hours or frozen for up to 1 week.

SPICY SEA BASS WITH FORBIDDEN RICE

2 shallots, thinly sliced
2 tablespoons olive oil
4 ounces roasted red chile paste
1 (13-ounce) can coconut milk
2 tablespoons freshly ground ginger
1 cup black forbidden rice
Vegetable broth or chicken broth
2 pounds center-cut sea bass or other flaky
    white fish, cut into 4 portions
Salt and pepper to taste
12 ounces baby arugula
2 tablespoons fresh lemon juice
1/4 cup chopped green onion tops

Serves 4

Sauté the shallots in the olive oil in a saucepan over medium-high heat until light brown. Stir in the chile paste and coconut milk. Simmer for 20 minutes or until reduced by one-third, stirring frequently. Stir in the ginger. Cook the rice according to the package directions, substituting the broth for water. Season the fish lightly with salt and pepper and place in a nonstick baking pan. Bake in a preheated 450-degree oven for 12 minutes or until the fish begins to flake. Toss the arugula and lemon juice in a bowl to mix. Serve the fish over rice. Spoon the sauce liberally over the top and arrange the arugula next to the fish. Sprinkle with the green onions.

Surprise your guests by serving the Spicy Sea Bass on black forbidden rice, a medium-size grain with a roasted nutty taste and deep purple color. Once eaten only by the emperors of China to increase health and longevity, the rice is high in antioxidants and iron, not to mention it makes a beautiful contrast on the plate. Make your guests feel like royalty and swap out regular rice for black forbidden rice at your next dinner party.

SWEETHEART HAZELNUT MOUSSE

1/2 cup chocolate hazelnut spread
1/2 teaspoon espresso powder
1 cup heavy whipping cream
Whipped cream for garnish
Fresh raspberries for garnish

Serves 4

*M*ix the hazelnut spread and espresso powder in a microwave-safe bowl. Microwave on High until smooth, stirring every 30 seconds. Whip the cream in a chilled bowl until stiff peaks form. Fold the hazelnut mixture into the whipped cream. Spoon into dessert bowls and garnish with whipped cream and raspberries.

Variation: You may use decorative cookies or fruit instead of garnishing with whipped cream.

GINGER CHAMPAGNE

1/2 cup chopped fresh ginger
2/3 cup sugar
1/2 cup water
3 tablespoons crystallized ginger, chopped
8 whole star anise
1 (750-milliliter) bottle of Champagne or
    sparkling wine

Serves 8

*B*ring the fresh ginger, sugar and water to a boil in a small saucepan. Reduce to a simmer. Cook for 15 minutes or until liquid thickens to maple syrup consistency. Remove from heat and let cool. Strain the syrup, discarding the ginger. Drop 1 teaspoon crystallized ginger and 1 star anise into each glass. Add 1 tablespoon syrup and top with about 3 ounces Champagne.

Note: Enjoy this cocktail with a spicy dish or appetizer. It also works well served at a holiday party.

Individual Bluegrass Gatherings Sponsors

Andrew and Sarah Barker

Joni and Kelly Burke

Leigh Burke-Schaad

Tiffany and Shawn Cardwell

Ashley L. Cassetty and Patsy Raymer

Madelyn Anetrella-Cerra

Barbara Cladwell and Jeremy Clark

Elizabeth Conway and Alice Baron

Mary Anne Cronan

Blair Crush

Philip and Rebecca Dydynski

Chrissy Evans

Ashley Alexander Hadley

Reid Hafer

Katherine L. Halloran

Emily James Hart

Heather E. Hise

Beth and Neil Hobson

Lisa Ann Holden

Susan and Brian Hovekamp

Linda Lu Jones

Mr. and Mrs. William A. Kantlehner, III

Aaron and Emily Kemp

Heather Kolasinsky

Jennifer Jenkins Kramer

Karen M. Le Blond

Blair Manning

Libby Milligan

Tifani Moore

Lisa Causarano Morley

Lisa W. Nash

Sissy Nash

Pia Posadas-Miller and Brian D. Miller

Kate Ratliff

Robin Rueff

Lauren Salome

Heather Schoolcraft

Monica Schroeder

Mrs. Carol E. Shannon

Amelia Smith

Angela Champion Sprowl

Keshia M. Swan

Carter Webb

Caroline Wells

Caroline and Warner Wheat

Michelle Black White

Hala Ziady

Junior League of Louisville
2012–2013 Leadership Council

President: Alice J. Baron

President Elect: Chrissy Evans

Sustainer Advisor: Hala Ziady

Community Advisor: Catherine Chapman

Diversity Advisor: Caroline Wheat

Fund Development Advisor: Libby Milligan

Membership/Leadership Advisor: Anita Barbee

VP Communications: Bethany Hobson

AVP Communications: Katherine Halloran

VP Community Impact: Christina Scott Weinstein

AVP Community Impact: Angela Champion Sprowl

VP Finance: Emily Hart

AVP Finance: Kathleen Reed

VP Fund-raising: Lauren Salome

AVP Fund-raising: Sarah B. Barker

VP Membership: Lisa Causarano Morley

Rec/Cor Secretary: Heather E. Hise

Member at Large: Blair Crush

VP Leadership Development and Education: Keshia Swan

Cookbook Committee

CO-CHAIRS

LaCinda Glover

Susan Hovekamp

SUB-COMMITTEE CHAIRS

Erica Downs	Lisa Causarano Morley	Heather Peterson
Reid Hafer	Lisa W. Nash	Monica Schroeder
Sarah Solberg Ludden	Lauren Ogden	Amelia Smith
Pia Posadas-Miller		Sara Smith

COMMITTEE MEMBERS

Kara Amore	Christina Gilles	Jennifer Jenkins Kramer
Judette Baylon	Erin Gish	Trish Lewellen
Nicole Bowen	Heather Berry Gough	Blair Manning
Mollie Bringhurst	Megan Harned	Michelle Moore
Tiffany Cardwell	Allison Hartley	Ann Baker Phillips
Anna Conley	Leah Hawkins	Kelly Choate Proud
Abigail Derr	Lisa Ann Holden	Kate Ratliff
Rebecca Dydynski	Janal Hughes	Colleen Rice
Camilla Earl	Ann Isaacs	Robin Rueff
Stephanie English	Emily Kemp	Julia Wayne
Katherine Giles		Chris Wicht

The Committee and the League would like to thank everyone who took time out of their busy lives to contribute and prepare recipes for our cookbook. We truly could not have done it without your generosity. Our sincere apologies go out to any gracious supporters who may have been unintentionally left off the list of contributors on pages 200 and 201. From our kitchen to yours—The Junior League of Louisville.

Farm Glossary

1. *Ashbourne Farms,* in La Grange, Kentucky, runs their farm as if they were raising food for their own family. They pasture graze their animals, free of antibiotics and hormones, to ensure that their wholesome beef, pork, and eggs are the highest quality protein. A commitment to sustainable agriculture and wildlife stewardship ensures that Ashbourne Farms respects the delicate balance of the land and those of us who inhabit it. 502-222-0852 www.ashbournefarms.com

2. *Barr Farms,* in Rhodelia, Kentucky, is a seventh generation family farm that prides themselves on raising produce. Greens, heirloom tomatoes, squash, okra, sweet potatoes, winter squash, broccoli, cabbage, onions, garlic, and many other vegetables are grown for CSA (Community Supported Agriculture) and farmers' markets. They also raise eggs, pastured chicken, and grass-fed beef. Food is raised with the intention of taking care of the land: healthy soil, healthy plants, healthy animals, and healthy people. 859-608-6458 www.barrfarmsky.com

3. *Capriole Farmstead,* in Greenville, Indiana, makes fresh, ripened, and aged chevres by hand, using only the milk of their own herd. This is a way of life in which the land and the animals manage their product. Fortune (or the lack of it) has truly given those at Capriole Farmstead a sense of who they are in relation to the wildness around them, respect for the animals that demand and give so much, and for the exacting craft of cheesemaking. 812-923-9408 www.capriolegoatcheese.com

4. *Col. Bill Newsom's Ham,* located in Princeton, Kentucky, is among the finest dry-cured hams in the world. Newsom's authentic, aged Kentucky country ham is a gourmet and country delicacy. Newsom's also offers smoked sausage, smoked bacon, preserves, breakfast mixes, sorghum molasses, dressings, relish, unprocessed wild honey, gourmet pickled vegetables, candies, cobblers, and a wide variety of cookbooks. 270-365-2482 www.newsomscountryham.com

5. *Courtney Farms,* in Bagdad, Kentucky, takes a lot of pride in its farming. The farm was purchased in 2006 and was a traditional tobacco farm for two years before they began to diversify their crop. They began raising produce in response to a community need for nutritious, local food—delivered. 502-747-0379 www.courtneyfarmscsa.com

6. *Four Hills Farm,* in Salvisa, Kentucky, raises Kathadin sheep. These sheep have been refined through years of breeding to produce mild-flavored, gourmet quality meat from a pasture-based production system. They call their Katahdin lamb the "New American Lamb" because it is believed they are a unique and upcoming breed offering many favorable attributes to the American lamb market. 859-865-4962 www.fourhillsfarm.com

7. *Foxhollow Farm,* in Crestwood, Kentucky, is a bio-dynamic farm community that provides healthy food while being a place where people can experience an earth-friendly, working farm. In addition to a wide variety of produce, Foxhollow Farm sells grass-fed beef. Grass-fed beef is healthier for the earth and the animals. It is also healthier for the consumer, as it is low in calories and saturated fat; high in Omega 3 fatty acids, Vitamin A and Vitamin E; and rich in protein. 502-241-9674 www.foxhollow.com

8. *Grateful Greens,* located just five minutes north of downtown Louisville, in Clarksville, Indiana, is a hydroponic lettuce and herb farm. They operate out of an 18,000-square- foot greenhouse, growing approximately 35,000 plants at a given time. The greenhouse is cycled fourteen times over the course of a year, which results in an annual production of

almost a half million plants. They also offer a wide variety of micro greens, pea shoots, wheatgrass, heirloom tomatoes, and edible flowers. 502-727-2572 www.gratefulgreensproduce.com

9. *Huber's Orchard and Winery,* located in Starlight, Indiana, has 600 acres of orchards and vineyards. The farmers' market features a large variety of fruits and vegetables but many patrons prefer the "u-pick" option. The gift shop features homemade apple butter, preserves, jams, jellies, cheeses, and much more. The barnyard offers numerous activities for children, and the family restaurant features many made-from-scratch favorites. With an ice cream factory, a winery that produces award-winning wines, and a distillery, this seventh generation family-owned farm truly has something for everyone. 812-923-5255 www.joehubers.com

10. *JD Country Milk,* in Logan County, Kentucky, is a family-owned and operated dairy farm and processing plant dedicated to providing quality hormone-free milk. Their cows are pasture-grazed and not given antibiotics or hormones. Their cows are also fed a vitamin-enriched diet and all the grass they can eat. With this type of care, JD Country Milk is some of the freshest and most delicious milk Kentuckians can enjoy. 270-726-2200 www.jdcountrymilk.com

11. *Kentucky Bison Co.,* in Goshen, Kentucky, proudly raises their buffalo on Woodland Farm without the use of steroids, stimulants, or sub-therapeutic antibiotics. Their herd includes several award-winning buffalo from top shows and sales in the United States as well as Canada. The foundation of Kentucky Bison Co. is based on the production, preservation, and promotion of the Authentic American Buffalo™. 877-859-2426 www.kybisonco.com

12. *Marksbury Farm Market,* in Lancaster, Kentucky, is a small-scale, locally owned butchers shop, farm market, and processing facility. They partner with local farmers who share their commitment to sustainable, humane, and natural production methods. Through their processing facility, they deliver an array of high-quality, healthy, and fresh products. 859-754-4224 www.marksburyfarm.com

13. *Smith Berry Vineyard and Winery,* in Henry County, Kentucky, has transitioned from a burley tobacco and milking farm to a company dedicated to grape-growing and winemaking, organic beef cattle, sheep, and hay crops. Smith Berry was established 1981, and they take great pride in raising organic vegetables for the residing family and for dinner and concert events throughout the summer. 502-845-7091 www.smithberrywinery.com

14. *Stone Cross Farm and Cloverdale Creamery,* in Taylorsville, Kentucky, is not just a business; it is a way of life. The family-run farm evolved from a successful dairy, beef cattle, and grain operation to a farm dedicated to the production of all-natural beef, pork, cheese, and soap products. They use only the best of what they know are safe, sustainable farming practices. 502-477-8561 www.stonecrossfarm.com

15. *Weisenberger Flour Mill* has been "the baker's choice" since 1865. Owned and operated for six generations by the Weisenberger family, the mill is nestled on banks of the South Elkhorn Creek, near Midway, in the heart of central Kentucky. They take great pride in the quality of their products as evidenced by their unconditional guarantee. 859-254-5282 www.weisenberger.com

The majority of these farms are Kentucky Proud.

Kentucky Produce Guide

Buying Kentucky Proud is easy. Look for the label at your grocery store, farmers' market, or roadside stand. Our secret ingredient is the hard work and dedication of Kentucky's farm families. Find out why "Nothing else is close."

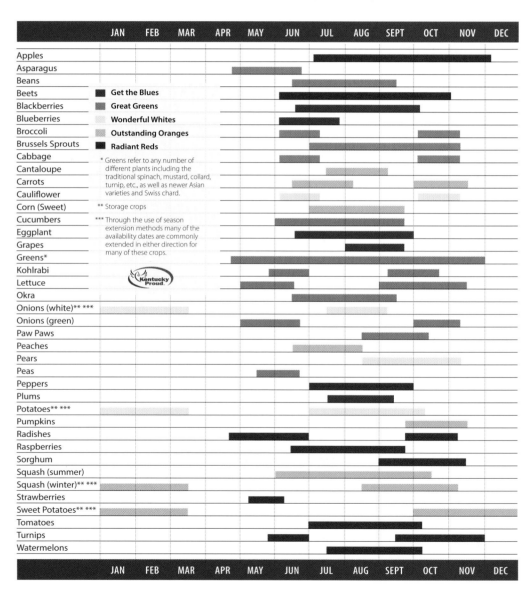

	JAN	FEB	MAR	APR	MAY	JUN	JUL	AUG	SEPT	OCT	NOV	DEC
Apples							■	■	■	■	■	
Asparagus				■	■	■						
Beans						■	■	■	■			
Beets						■	■	■	■	■	■	
Blackberries						■	■	■	■			
Blueberries						■	■					
Broccoli						■	■			■	■	
Brussels Sprouts							■	■	■	■		
Cabbage							■	■	■	■		
Cantaloupe							■	■				
Carrots							■	■	■	■	■	
Cauliflower							■	■	■			
Corn (Sweet)							■	■	■			
Cucumbers						■	■	■	■			
Eggplant						■	■	■	■			
Grapes								■	■			
Greens*				■	■	■	■	■	■	■	■	
Kohlrabi						■	■		■	■		
Lettuce					■	■			■	■	■	
Okra							■	■	■			
Onions (white)** ***	■	■	■				■	■	■			
Onions (green)					■	■	■	■	■	■		
Paw Paws									■	■		
Peaches						■	■	■				
Pears									■	■	■	
Peas					■	■						
Peppers							■	■	■	■		
Plums							■	■	■			
Potatoes** ***	■	■	■				■	■	■			
Pumpkins									■	■	■	
Radishes					■	■	■		■	■		
Raspberries						■	■	■	■	■		
Sorghum									■	■	■	
Squash (summer)						■	■	■	■	■		
Squash (winter)** ***	■	■	■					■	■	■		
Strawberries					■	■						
Sweet Potatoes** ***	■	■	■						■	■	■	■
Tomatoes							■	■	■	■		
Turnips						■	■		■	■	■	
Watermelons							■	■	■			

Legend:
- ■ Get the Blues
- ■ Great Greens
- ■ Wonderful Whites
- ■ Outstanding Oranges
- ■ Radiant Reds

* Greens refer to any number of different plants including the traditional spinach, mustard, collard, turnip, etc., as well as newer Asian varieties and Swiss chard.

** Storage crops

*** Through the use of season extension methods many of the availability dates are commonly extended in either direction for many of these crops.

Wine Pairings

MENU	WINE PAIRINGS

SPRING

March Madness — Medium-bodied, dry Pinot Noir from California

April Showers Bring May Flowers — Dry, medium-bodied, crisp Grüner Veltliner from Austria

Thunder Cookout — Dry, light and crisp Sauvignon Blanc from New Zealand

Lilies for the Fillies Cocktail Party — Dry, full-bodied red wine from Côtes Du Rhône

Run for the Roses Brunch — Dry, light and crisp Austrian Riesling, or sweet, light Moscato D'Asti from Italy

SUMMER

Patio Wine Party — Dry, medium-bodied Rioja Crianza from Spain

On the Grill — Dry, light Pinot Noir from Oregon

Bastille Day — Dry, crisp Cru Beaujolais Brouilly

Farmers' Market — Dry, medium-bodied Dolcetto from Italy

Cool Down Salad Party — Dry, fruity and floral Torrontes from Argentina

FALL

Tailgating — Dry, rich, full-bodied Malbec from Argentina

St. James Court Art Show — Dry, medium-bodied, rich Riesling from Alsace, France

Oktoberfest — Dry, light and crisp Grüner Veltliner from Austria

Breeders' Cup Brunch — Dry, medium-bodied Chardonnay from Oregon

Harvest Dinner — Dry, medium-bodied, crisp Pinot Noir from Burgundy, France

WINTER

Holiday Cocktail Party — Dry, crisp sparkling Prosecco from Italy

New Year's Day — Dry, light and fruity Beaujolais-Village from Burgundy, France

Soup Night — Light, crisp and dry Verdicchio from Italy

Snow Day — Dry, medium-bodied Chianti Classico from Italy

Valentine's Day Dinner — Dry, medium-bodied Albarino from Spain

—Scott Harper, MS; Managing Partner and Corporate Wine and Beverage Director, Bristol Bar & Grille

Recipe Preparers and Contributors

Sharon Adams
Cindy Adelberg
Ruthie Alexander
Kori Andrews
Madelyn Anetrella-Cerra
Michelle Arnold
Laura Baker
Alice J. Baron
Judette Baylon
Betsy Becker
Meredith Belew
Megan Bertucci
Jane Beshear
Eunice F. Blocker
Marian Boncato
Liz Bornwasser
Joyce Bosco
Jacquelyn Bowman
Kelley Bright
Mollie Bringhurst
Nancye Brown
Elizabeth Bruenderman
Melissa Buddeke
Missy Burge
Rachel Busby
Tiffany Cardwell
Karen Casi
Ashley L. Cassetty
John Castro
Josef Causarano
Mary Cheatham
Christine Chiu
Meredith Clipp-Rodriquez
Teresa Coburn
Dana Cohen
Anna Conley
Lynn Thompson Connolly
Elizabeth Conway
Anne Coorssen
Donna Coots
Courtney Cornett
Selina J. Costley
Bree Couch

Laura Crahan
Alison Cromer
Ashley Crutcher
Lisa DeJaco Crutcher
Marc Crutcher
Bridget Dale
Cate Darmstadt
Sally Davenport
Kelly Davis
Mallory Day
Shannon De'Domenico
Tara Denahm
Deborah Denyul
Candace Depp
Stacy Dickens
Ellen Diebold
Richard Doering
Caroline Dowell
Elizabeth Dowell
Erica Downs
Nancy Downs
Shirley Rankin Dumesnil
Marian Dunkerley
Rebecca Dydynski
Camilla Earl
Rachel Elliott
Stephanie English
Jamie Estes
Chrissy Evans
Georgia Farnan
Amanda Fehribach
Christi Fenton
Shelby Fink
Maria Fisher
Kelly Fleenor
Ann Fleming
Jenny Frachtman
Sarah Frey
Melissa Capito Fuchs
Carol Gates
Holly Gathright
Alexandra Gerassimides
Christina Gilles

LaCinda Glover
Heather Berry Gough
Beth Grammer
Ann Grant
Sally Gray
Danielle Greeson
Ashley Alexander Hadley
Reid Hafer
Ethel Hale
Megan Harned
Becca Haynes
Beth Hinkebein
Heather E. Hise
Beth Hobson
Sarah Hoffman
Lisa Ann Holden
Patty Hooker
Cathy Hovekamp
Cheri Hovekamp
Susan Hovekamp
Lynn Howard
Sarah Howard
Sarah Huelsman
Janal Hughes
Ruth Hughes
Linda Hunt
Regan Hunt
Ann Isaacs
Olga Itkin
Judy Jenkins
Linda Lu Jones
Lindsay Jones
Stephanie Kaebrick
Patty Kantlehner
Rebecca Keinsley
Anne Keller
Emily Kemp
JJ Kingery
Peachy Kohler
Heather Kolasinsky
Mary Kovalesky
Jennifer Jenkins Kramer
Janet Krantz

Man Yan Lam
Jennifer Lasky
Karen M. Le Blond
Danatta Levine
Trish Lewellen
Carolyn Lewis
Sarah Solberg Ludden
Sarah Lutrell
Blair Manning
Caroline Mapother
Meaghan Marrett
Marilyn Martin-Phillips
Kristen Mauer
Whitney McAnally
Susan McCampbell
Leah McComb
Alice McKinley
Annie McLaughlin
Tess McNair
Rebecca McNeily
Anne Miller
Elizabeth Miller
Pam Miller
Delaurah Minzenberger
Lisa Causarano Morley
Michelle Moore
Betty Moorman
Maria Morozowich
Erica Morris
Rachel Mueller
Lisa W. Nash
Nicole Bremer Nash
Sissy Nash
Sallie Niehoff
Aneesah Nu'Man
Kyle O'Donnell
Lauren Ogden
Beth Orberson
Kathy Oyler
Nicole Pang
Megan Parker
Margaret Payne
Cheryl Perry

Sally Perry
Fran Peters
Heather Peterson
Joy Philbin
Ann Baker Phillips
Susan D. Phillips
Stephanie Pieper-Reilly
Jacquelyn Pobst
Pia Posadas-Miller
Sandra Proctor
Laura Pruniski
Lindsay Pruniski
Alexis Raley
Martie Rankin
Beth Ratliff
Kate Ratliff
Melissa Richards-Person
Carly Rider
Monica Rinaudo
Sandy Rogers
Rich Rosenberg

Leslie Rueff
Robin Rueff
Helen Grace Ryan
Whitney Ryan
Lauren Salome
Lauren Sappenfield
Judy Schad
Andrea Scholtz
Amy Schrader
Monica Schroeder
Sarah Seadler
Rachel Segretto
Marilyn Collis Sexton
Carol E. Shannon
Carolyn Sheldon
Linda Shepard
Amelia Smith
Amy Smith
Sara Smith
Sara Sowder
Laura Spalding

LaShawnda Speck
Shawnda Speck
Angela Champion Sprowl
Robin Stanback
Cathy Stopher
Louis Straub
Mary Sullivan
Keshia M. Swan
Kate Talamini
Jean Terry
Jessica Thompson
Kenisha Thompson
Melanie Thornton
Susie Toso
Allison Truman
Lisa Tyler
Kimberly Ulrich
Patty Von Allmen
Trish Wallace
Brittany Warren
Julia Wayne

Hunter Weinberg
Christina Scott Weinstein
Eddie Wells
Terry Wise Wells
Christine Wernert
Emily Wharton
Caroline Wheat
Jessica Whirt
Michelle Black White
Chris Wicht
Mary Ellen Wiederwohl
Dianne Wininger
Harriet Wood
Annalee Cato Worthington
Jean Wright
Tara Lewis Wurdock
Noell Yanik
Kelly Youngblook
Hala Ziady

Chef Contributors

Chef Casey Broussard	Wiltshire Pantry ✳
Chef Kathy Cary	Lilly's—A Kentucky Bistro ✳
Chef Dean Corbett	Corbett's—an American place ✳
Chef Claudia Delatorre	Cake Flour—A Natural Baking Company ✳
Chef Alexander Dulaney	Bistro Le Relais ✳
Sarah Fritschner	Louisville Farm to Table
Chef Laurent Géroli	The Brown Hotel
Master Sommelier Scott Harper	Bristol Bar & Grille ✳
Chef Anthony Lamas	Seviche
Toni Lavenson	VINT Coffee
Chef Tyson Long	Sullivan University & Winston's Restarant ✳
Chef Ghyslain Maurais	Ghyslain
Chef Brian Morgan	Eiderdown ✳
Joy Perrine	Jack's Lounge
Chef Michael Ton	Doc Crow's Southern Smokehouse & Raw Bar
Chef Brian Ucán	Mayan Café ✳
Chef Levon Wallace	Proof on Main ✳
Chef Shawn Ward	Jack Fry's ✳
Chef from deSha's	deSha's

✳ Denotes Kentucky Proud Restaurant

201

Index

Bluegrass Gatherings

Entertaining Through Kentucky's Seasons

To order additional copies of
Bluegrass Gatherings
visit our website at:
www.juniorleaguelouisville.org

Or contact us at:
Junior League of Louisville
982 Eastern Parkway Suite 7
Louisville, Kentucky 40217
502-637-5415

For more information on photography, visit:

Fred Minnick	M. A. Buckner
www.fredphoto.net	www.mabuckner.com